Excellent English 3
Language Skills for Success
WORKBOOK

Mary Ann Maynard
Ingrid Wisniewska

Jan Forstrom
Marta Pitt
Shirley Velasco

Excellent English Workbook 3

Published by McGraw-Hill ESL/ELT, a business unit of The McGraw-Hill Companies, Inc.1221 Avenue of the Americas, New York, NY 10020. Copyright © 2008 by The McGraw-Hill Companies, Inc. All rights reserved. No part of this publication may be reproduced or distributed in any form or by any means, or stored in a database or retrieval system, without the prior written consent of The McGraw-Hill Companies, Inc., including, but not limited to, any network or other electronic storage or transmission, or broadcast for distance learning.

Printed in the United States of America.

ISBN 13: 978-0-07-719393-5 (Workbook)
ISBN 10: 0-07-719393-8
6 7 8 9 10 QDB 12

Series editor: Nancy Jordan
Developmental editors: Nancy Jordan, Eve Einselen
Production manager: Juanita Thompson
Cover designer: Witz End Design
Interior designer: NETS

Illustrators: Punto 5 Graphic Design, Silvia Plata, Ismael Sanchez

Photo credits:

Page 6: Somos/Veer/Getty Images; ThinkStock/SuperStock; Christina Kennedy/Getty Images; **Page 9:** Digital Vision Ltd./SuperStock; Pixtal/SuperStock; **Page 11:** PhotoAlto/Sigrid Olsson/Getty; **Page 13:** Brand X/SuperStock; **Page 16:** David Bacon/The Image Works; image100/SuperStock; Douglas Kirkland/CORBIS; **Page 20:** SSPL/The Image Works; GK Hart/Vicky Hart/Getty Images; Comstock/SuperStock; Tobi Zausner; Corbis/SuperStock; Photodisc/SuperStock; **Page 22:** Clive Streeter/Getty Images; Dynamic Graphics Value/SuperStock; **Page 27:** Digital Vision Ltd./SuperStock; **Page 28:** D. Hurst/Alamy; Photodisc/SuperStock; Stockbyte/SuperStock; **Page 30:** James J. Bissell/SuperStock; Blend Images/SuperStock; Digital Vision Ltd./SuperStock; Helene Rogers/Alamy; **Page 35:** INSADCO Photography/Alamy; **Page 36:** David R. Frazier/The Image Works; Tobi Zausner; Blend Images/SuperStock; **Page 40:** XXX; **Page 42:** Image Source Black/Alamy; Wm. Baker/GhostWorx Images/Alamy; Kitt Cooper-Smith/Alamy; age fotostock/SuperStock; **Page 45:** Onoky/SuperStock; **Page 50:** Image Source/SuperStock; Odilon Dimier/Getty Image; **Page 51:** altrendo images/Getty Images; **Page 52:** Corbis/SuperStock; Art Kowalsky/Alamy; James Lemass/SuperStock; **Page 54:** Jim Craigmyle/ Corbis; **Page 56:** age fotostock/SuperStock; **Page 59:** BananaStock/SuperStock; Photodisc/SuperStock; **Page 64:** Custom Medical Stock Photo/Alamy; **Page 65:** Hurewitz Creative/Corbis; **Page 66:** Tobi Zausner; Garry Gay/Alamy ABXAEC; Dennis MacDonald/Alamy; Mediscan/Corbis; **Page 70:** Siri Stafford/Getty Images; **Page 82:** Masterfile; Phil Degginger/Alamy; Digital Vision/Alamy; **Page 83:** Comstock Select/Corbis; **Page 92:** Image Source Pink/Alamy; VStock/Alamy; ThinkStock/SuperStock; **Page 96:** Mitch Wojnarowicz/Amsterdam Recorder/The Image Works; Ray Manley/SuperStock; Corbis/SuperStock; Historic NWS Collection/NOAA; Ingram Publishing (Superstock Limited)/Alamy; **Page 100:** Lourens Smak/Alamy; **Page 107:** Blend Images/Alamy; **Page 114:** BananaStock/SuperStock; Somos/Veer/Getty Images; Photodisc/SuperStock; Big Cheese Photo/SuperStock; **Page 119:** Image Source Pink/Getty Images; Photodisc/Alamy; JLP/Jose L. Pelaez/Corbis; Judith Collins/Alamy; GK Hart/Vikki Hart/Getty Images; Lew Robertson/Corbis; **Page 120:** Image Source Black/Getty Images; Robert Manella/Comstock/Corbis; Purestock/Getty Images; Jose Luis Pelaez Inc/Blend Images/Corbis; **Page 124:** Digital Vision/Getty Images; **Page 142:** Purestock/SuperStock; **Page 149:** Image Source Pink/ Getty Images; Altrendo images/Getty Images; **Page 151:** Stockbyte/SuperStock; **Page 154:** Kevin Radford/SuperStock; **Page 163:** age fotostock/SuperStock; **Page 171:** Image Source Pink/SuperStock

Cover photo:
Hand: Getty
Dentist: Corbis
Smiling family: Corbis
Business woman: Corbis
Graduate: Corbis

 **McGraw-Hill**

To the Teacher

PROGRAM OVERVIEW

> **Excellent English: Language Skills for Success** equips students with the grammar and skills they need to access community resources while developing the foundation for long-term career and academic success.

Excellent English is a four-level, grammar-oriented series for English learners featuring a *Grammar Picture Dictionary* approach to vocabulary building and grammar acquisition. An accessible and predictable sequence of lessons in each unit systematically builds language and math skills around life-skill topics. *Excellent English* is tightly correlated to all of the major standards for adult instruction.

- CASAS (the Comprehensive Adult Student Assessment Systems)
- Los Angeles Unified School District's Competency-Based Education (CBE) Course Outlines
- Florida Adult ESOL Syllabi
- EFF (Equipped for the Future) Content Standards
- SCANS (Secretary's Commission on Achieving Necessary Skills)

The Excellent English Workbook with Audio CD is an essential companion to the Student Book. Each workbook unit provides 14 pages of supplementary practice for its corresponding Student Book unit. The Workbook provides students with further practice with the grammar, vocabulary, listening, reading, writing, and life-skill competencies taught in the Student Book. It offers application lessons that cover competencies in addition to those that are covered in the Student Book.

Features

- **Family Connection** and **Community Connection** lessons provide practice with additional competencies related to the topic of each Student Book unit.

- **Career Connection** lessons build off the Career Connection photo story in the Student Book and address additional work-related competencies.

- **Technology Connection** lessons introduce students to technology objectives as they are used in everyday life, such as using voicemail or filling out an online job application.

- **Culture and Communication** activities introduce culturally appropriate communication strategies, such as using various levels of formality or asking for and giving advice, Culture Tips provide additional useful cultural information.

- **Real-Life Lessons** take learning beyond the classroom as students use new language skills to gather information about their own community through interviews and research.

- **Practice tests** in every unit, complete with CASAS-type listening tasks from the Workbook CD, encourage students to test their skills in a low-stakes environment.

- An **Audio CD**—packaged with each Workbook— includes recorded passages for the Listening and Conversation lesson and Pronunciation activities, as well as for the practice tests.

Contents

Pre-unit

Unit 1

STUDY SKILLS AND LEARNING STYLES

Unit 2

GET VALUE FOR YOUR MONEY

Unit 3

TRAFFIC AND WORK SAFETY

Unit 4

LAWS, RULES, AND REGULATIONS

Unit 5

STAYING HEALTHY

Unit 6

GETTING INVOLVED IN YOUR COMMUNITY

Unit 7

OUR ENVIRONMENT

Unit 8

SERVICES IN YOUR COMMUNITY

Unit 9

GETTING BUSY

Unit 10

SOLVING PROBLEMS

Unit 11

MOVING OUT AND MOVING IN

Unit 12

LIFE MILESTONES

Language in the Classroom

1 **LISTEN** and complete the conversation. Use the words and phrases in the box.

WCD, 2

| class | let me introduce you | meet you | My name | new student | Nice to |

Dan: Hi. I'm Dan. Are you a (1) ___new student_____?

Sue: Yes, I am. (2) _____is Sue.

Dan: Nice to (3) _____, Sue.

Sue: Dan, (4) _____to another student in this class. This is Ana.

Ana: Nice to meet you, Dan. Welcome to our (5) _____.

Dan: Thank you, Ana. (6) _____meet you, too.

2 **WRITE** a conversation. Introduce yourself to two of your classmates. Write in your notebook.

3 **PRACTICE** the conversation you wrote in Activity 2 with two partners.

4 **WRITE.** Number the lines of the conversations in the correct order.

1.

_____ *Dave:* Okay. I'll be Student B. You start.

_____ *Dave:* Sure, Sara. My name is Dave.

_____ *Sara:* Hi. I'm Sara. Would you be my partner?

_____ *Sara:* Nice to meet you, Dave. I'll be Student A.

2.

_____ *Dave:* It's your turn.

_____ *Sara:* Okay, whose turn is it, now?

_____ *Dave:* Okay. I'll be Student A now.

_____ *Sara:* Let's switch roles.

5 **MATCH** the questions and the answers.

_c_ 1. What is your name?

____ 2. Where are you from?

____ 3. Are you a new student?

____ 4. What language do you speak?

____ 5. When did you move here?

a. I'm from Mexico.

b. Two years ago.

c. ~~Maria.~~

e. Yes, I am.

f. Spanish.

6 **LISTEN.** Complete the conversation. Use the words and expressions in the box.

WCD, 3

Did you say	~~My name is~~	repeat that	spell that	That's right	you live

Dave: Are you a new student?

Maria: Yes, I am. (1) ___My name is_____Maria Ramirez.

Dave: (2) _____Ramirez?

Maria: (3) _____.

Dave: Could you (4) _____, please?

Maria: R-A-M-I-R-E-Z. What's your name?

Dave: Dave Green.

Maria: Nice to meet you , Dave. Where do (5) _____?

Dave: I live on Pine Street.

Maria: Excuse me, could you (6) _____, please?

Dave: Sure. I live on Pine Street.

7 **PRACTICE.** Talk with a partner. Use the phrases in the box. Then switch roles.

Student A	Student B
What is your name?	Can you please repeat that?
How do you spell that?	Did you say…?
Where do you live?	Could you please say that again?
Did you say…?	Do you understand what I said?
Can you please repeat that?	Let's switch roles.
What language do you speak?	

Grammar Review

1 MATCH the questions and the answers. Then write the correct **bold** words next to the grammar word.

1. Where is **the** library? __c__

2. Where **do** you shop? ____

3. Are you **married**? ____

4. How many people are in your **family**? ____

a. I **usually** shop at the Good Food Store.

b. There are six people **in** my family.

c. The library **is** on Pine Street.

d. No, **I** am single.

adjective	helping /auxiliary verb	preposition	article
married	_____	_____	_____

adverb	main verb	pronoun	noun
_____	_____	_____	_____

2 COMPLETE. Read the paragraph. Match the verbs in **bold** with the correct verb form.

a. simple past	b. present continuous	c. future with *be going to*	d. simple present	e. future with *will*

Ana Ramirez **moved** (1) ____a____ here last year. She **attends** (2) _____ the Greenville Adult School five days a week. Right now, she**'s studying** (3) _____ English. She**'s going to study** (4) _____ business at the community college this fall. She**'ll get** (5) _____ a job as an office manager next year.

3 WRITE each sentence in Activity 2 in the negative form. Write in your notebook.

Example: *Ana Ramirez didn't move here last year.*

4 MATCH the mistakes in the paragraph with the type of mistake in the box.

__d__ punctuation	_____ spelling	_____ verb form	_____ capitalization

My name is Dave Green. I'm a student at the community colege. Last year, I take English classes.
                                                 a.   **b.**
right now, Im taking nursing classes. I want to get a job as a nurse. My classes are interesting, and
c.   **d.**
I am learning a lot.

Use Your Dictionary

1 **READ** the definitions of *teach* and *teacher* from the dictionary. Then (circle) the correct answer to each question below.

> **teach** /tich/ *v.* to give lessons or instructions to someone: *I teach ESL students at the adult school this year.*
>
> **tea•cher** /ˈtichur/ *n.* a person who gives lessons or instructions to someone: *Our teacher gave us homework today.*

1. What part of speech is *teach*?　　　　　a. noun　b. verb　c. adjective　d. adverb

2. How many syllables does *teach* have?　　a. one　b. two　c. three　d. four

3. What part of speech is *teacher*?　　　　a. noun　b. verb　c. adjective　d. adverb

4. How many syllables does *teacher* have?　a. one　b. two　c. three　d. four

5. Which syllable is stressed in *teacher*?　a. first　b. second　c. third　d. fourth

2 **USE YOUR DICTIONARY.** Complete the chart.

	What part of speech is it?	How many syllables are there?	Which syllable is stressed?
activity	noun	4	second
attend			
football			
seriously			
specific			

Lesson 1

1 **COMPLETE** the sentences. Use the words in the box.

academic counselor	lab assistant	office hours	study group	~~tour~~	tutor

1. The new students are taking a _____*tour*_____ of the school library.

2. Ann is meeting with her _____ to get help with her assignment.

3. Sara asks her _____ for advice on her goals.

4. Greg makes an appointment to see the instructor during _____ .

5. The _____ can show you how to use the computer.

6. I meet with other students in my _____ after class on Fridays.

2 **COMPLETE** the sentences. Write the verb in the simple present or the present continuous.

1. (study) Matt _____*is studying*_____ now.

2. (not, talk) I _____ usually _____ to my academic counselor every week.

3. (write) Ella and Hong _____ an assignment right now.

4. (sit) Steve _____ in the same place every day.

5. (not, come) You _____ often _____ to class on time.

6. (not, listen) Ray _____ to the instructor right now.

3 **COMPLETE** the sentences. Use the words in the box and the correct form of the verbs.

academic counselor	librarian	tutor

1. Kate is a _____*librarian*_____. She _____ (give) a tour right now.
   She usually _____ (work) in the library every day.

2. Sam is a _____. He _____ (help) a student with
   an assignment right now. He usually _____ (meet) each student once a week.

3. Bernie is an _____. He _____ (talk) a student
   right now. He usually _____ (see) each student once every semester.

Lesson 2

1 COMPLETE the story. Write the correct form of the verb. Use simple present or present continuous.

It's 4:30 P.M. and the students (1) ___are finishing___ (finish) their English

class. Mrs. Stevens, the instructor, (2) _____ (explain) the homework

assignment right now. Most of the students (3) _____ (listen)

carefully. Jen (4) _____ (take) notes now. She's an excellent student

and she always (5) _____ (get) excellent grades for her assignments.

Rick (6) _____ (highlight) important words in his textbook right now.

He (7) _____ (not always, understand) the instructions, and he usually

(8) _____ (ask) a few questions at the end of the class. Ling and

Emmy (9) _____ (talk) in the back of the class right now. They

rarely (10) _____ (do) their homework on time. Mrs. Stevens

sometimes (11) _____ (get) upset because their homework is late.

I (12) _____ (draw) illustrations of new words in my notebook right

now. I'll ask my study group about the homework later.

2 MATCH the questions with the answers.

_c_ 1. What is Mrs. Stevens doing?

____ 2. Is Jen taking notes?

____ 3. What are the students doing?

____ 4. Are Ling and Emmy listening?

____ 5. What is Rick doing?

____ 6. Is Rick asking a question?

a. He's highlighting new words.

b. No, they aren't.

c. ~~She's explaining the homework.~~

d. No, he isn't.

e. They're listening to the instructor.

f. Yes, she is.

 3 WRITE a description of the students in your class. What are they doing (or not doing) right now?

Lesson 3

1 LISTEN to the question. Then listen to the conversation. Listen to the question again. Fill in the circle for the correct answer.

1. Ⓐ Ⓑ Ⓒ   2. Ⓐ Ⓑ Ⓒ   3. Ⓐ Ⓑ Ⓒ

2 LISTEN. Check ☑ the learning strategies you hear. Which of these strategies do you use?

☐ Draw illustrations   ☐ Meet with a study group

☐ Find resources in the library ☐ Schedule time to study

☐ Highlight words   ☐ Type notes

☐ Make flashcards   ☐ Write example sentences

3 MATH. Read Matt's schedule for the week. Then answer the questions.

Monday	study group 1-3 P.M. English class 3-6 P.M.	Tuesday	tutor 2-3 P.M. computer lab 3-5 P.M.	Wednesday	computer lab 1-3 P.M. English class 3-6 P.M.
Thursday	FREE	Friday	study group 1-3 P.M. English class 3-6 P.M.	Saturday	library

1. How many hours a week does Matt have English class? _____

2. How many hours a week does Matt meet with his study group? _____

3. How many hours a week does Matt go to computer lab? _____

4. How many hours a week is Matt at school? _____

4 NUMBER the lines of the conversation in the correct order.

___1___ A: Hi! How are you?

_____ B: Well, it was good to see you.

_____ B: Let's do that. I'll call you this weekend.

_____ B: Good. How are you?

_____ A: Okay. Great! See you!

_____ A: Great. I wish I could talk longer, but I'm on my way to class.

_____ A: Good to see you, too. Let's get together soon.

_____ B: Bye!

5 PRACTICE the conversation with a partner.

Culture and Communication: In the Classroom

1 **TALK** about the pictures with a partner. What are these teachers and students doing now? What do you think they usually do every day?

> ### Culture Tip
>
> In U.S. classrooms, students often work together in pairs or groups. This helps to give students more speaking practice. Students can learn from each other as well as from the teacher.

2 **READ** the sentences. Compare your school now and a school in another country. What do teachers and students usually do? Check ☑ your answers. Add your own ideas. Compare your answers with a partner.

	In the U.S.	In _____ (Name of country)
1. We ask the teacher questions.	☐	☐
2. The teacher asks us questions	☐	☐
3. We are quiet when the teacher is speaking.	☐	☐
4. The teacher corrects our mistakes.	☐	☐
5. Students talk in pairs or small groups.	☐	☐
6. We stand up when the teacher comes in.	☐	☐
7. We have homework every day.	☐	☐
8. The teacher corrects our homework.	☐	☐
9. _____	☐	☐
10. _____	☐	☐
11. _____	☐	☐
12. _____	☐	☐

 3 **WRITE** a description of your class. What do you usually do in class? What does the teacher usually do? What do you usually NOT do?

Lesson 4

1 **COMPLETE** the sentences. Use the words in the box.

| attended | priority | responsibility | set | stuck | support |

1. Allie ___attended___ every class. She was never absent.

2. Sam planned all his study time in his diary. He got up early and _____ to a schedule.

3. Marta's mother took care of Marta's daughter so Marta could do her homework. Marta got _____ from her family.

4. Tess tried to improve her study skills. She took _____ for learning.

5. Jon didn't play football or go to the gym this semester. He made learning a _____.

6. Wanda decided to learn five new words every day. She _____ goals for learning.

2 **WRITE** yes/no questions about the people in Activity 1. Then write short answers.

1. (Allie / attend every class) _Did Allie attend every class_ ? _Yes, she did_____.

2. (Sam / get up late) _____? _____.

3. (Marta / do her homework) _____? _____.

4. (Tess / motivated) _____? _____.

5. (Jon/ play football) _____? _____.

6. (Wanda / set goals) _____? _____.

3 **COMPLETE** the chart with information about yourself.

Are you going to…?	Yes/No	How?
take responsibility for learning?	Yes.	I'm going to meet with a tutor every week.
make learning a priority?		
set goals?		
be on time for every class?		
stick to a schedule?		
have support?		

4 **TALK.** Tell a partner about yourself. Use the information in your chart.

Example: I'm going to take responsibility for learning. For example, I'm going to meet with a tutor every week.

Lesson 5

1 **COMPLETE** the sentences. Use the words in the box.

complete	cooperate	courteous	motivated	~~pay attention~~	support

1. Please listen carefully. I want you to ___*pay attention*___.

2. Please work in a group. You will need to _____ with your classmates.

3. Please be friendly and _____ to the other students in this class.

4. Remember to _____ your homework on time.

5. Think about why English is important for you. That will help you to be _____.

6. You can ask a tutor in the academic advice center for _____.

2 **USE YOUR DICTIONARY.**

1. Write the words in the chart according to their syllable stress.

attention	complete	explanation	important	remember
~~classroom~~	courteous	homework	motivated	understand

1st syllable stressed	2nd syllable stressed	3rd syllable stressed
classroom		

2. Which words start with a vowel sound? _____

3. Which words start with a consonant sound? _____
   Practice the pronunciation.

3 **COMPLETE** the story.

   Francisco is unhappy. He doesn't do well on his homework and he doesn't
know why. He always writes the homework assignment in his notebook, but
then he forgets about it. He tries to finish it the night before class, but he often
doesn't understand the instructions. This semester he is going to do three things
to improve his homework grades. First, ___*he is going to read his homework assignments*___
carefully. Second, _____.
Third, _____.

Family Connection: Identifying Learning Styles

1 **READ** the questionnaire. Check ✓ your answers.

1. When you open a book or a magazine, do you usually…?
   - ☐ **a.** look at the pictures first
   - ☐ **b.** read the titles and chapter headings
   - ☐ **c.** look through the whole book or magazine before you start

2. When you read a book or a story, do you usually…?
   - ☐ **a.** see pictures in your mind
   - ☐ **b.** hear the sound of the words
   - ☐ **c.** imagine doing the actions in the story

3. When the teacher gives homework, do you usually prefer to…?
   - ☐ **a.** read the instructions
   - ☐ **b.** listen to the instructions
   - ☐ **c.** start the homework and ask questions later

4. When you learn new vocabulary, do you usually…?
   - ☐ **a.** draw pictures to remember them
   - ☐ **b.** say the words aloud many times
   - ☐ **c.** put words on pieces of paper around your room

5. When you write a homework assignment, do you usually…?
   - ☐ **a.** draw a chart of your ideas
   - ☐ **b.** talk to yourself about the topic
   - ☐ **c.** walk around the room while you are thinking

6. When you study for an exam, do you usually…?
   - ☐ **a.** make notes and highlight important information
   - ☐ **b.** read aloud from my notes or from the book
   - ☐ **c.** think of actions to go with important sentences or information

Add up your score

Total number of **a** answers: _____

Total number of **b** answers: _____

Total number of **c** answers: _____

2 **READ** the questions again.

If you had a lot of **a** answers, then you are a visual learner.
If you had a lot of **b** answers, then you are an auditory learner.
If you had a lot of **c** answers, then you are a kinesthetic learner.
Are you mainly visual, auditory, or kinesthetic in your learning style? Give some other examples.

3 **READ** the report cards for these children. Then answer the questions.

Teacher Comments:

Tina works well with her classmates. She is motivated and participates in all class activities. She enjoys music and listening to stories. She needs to improve her reading skills.

Teacher Comments:

Wei is shy and quiet in class. He reads well and his vocabulary is good for his age. He listens carefully and can follow instructions easily. He needs to cooperate more with other students in group tasks.

Teacher Comments:

Gabby is always courteous, cheerful, and helpful. She loves music and dance. In class, she sometimes has difficulty finishing her tasks. She needs to learn to sit quietly and pay attention.

1. Which learning style do you think each child has? (visual/auditory/kinesthetic)

Tina _____ Wei _____ Gabby _____

2. Identify ways for a parent to help each child improve study habits at home.

Tina should _____.

Wei should _____.

Gabby should _____.

4 **REAL-LIFE LESSON.** Work with a partner. Role-play a parent and a teacher talking about one of the children in Activity 3. Suggest ways to improve their study skills.

Example: *Parent:* How can Tina improve her study skills?

Teacher: She needs to improve her reading. Maybe you could read with her at home?

Community Connection: Making a Plan to Improve Your Community

1 THINK ABOUT IT. Read the notice. What is the purpose of this notice?

Join our Reading Group!

Join our reading group and meet new friends, learn from each other, and share opinions and ideas.

SCHEDULE: Our meetings are on the 4th Tuesday of every month from 6 to 9 P.M.
LOCATION: Public Library, downstairs meeting room
FIRST MEETING: January 24. Please bring suggestions for book titles to this meeting!

Coffee and cake will be served.

2 READ the paragraph. <u>Underline</u> the topic sentence and the concluding sentence. Draw a <u>wavy line</u> under the supporting sentences Draw a <u>dotted line</u> under the examples or details.

Our Neighborhood Reading Group

Our neighborhood reading group has three main goals. Our first goal is to read some interesting books and talk about them. We're going to choose six books and read one book every two months. Our second goal is to make friends and get to know each other. We want to build a happy neighborhood and community. Our third goal is to learn from each other. We can learn a lot by discussing our opinions. Our reading group is going to bring people together in our neighborhood.

3 **TALK** with a partner. Think of three goals to make your community a better place. Write the goals. Then give a detail or an example for each goal. You will use this information to write a paragraph.

Goal 1: _____

Detail: _____

Goal 2: _____

Detail: _____

Goal 3: _____

Detail: _____

4 **WRITE** a paragraph. Use your information in Activity 3. Follow the example in Activity 2.

5 **REAL-LIFE LESSON.** Find out about a community group in your neighborhood. What do they do? Where do they meet? How often? Write the information below.

Name of group _____

Activities _____

Location / Time of meetings _____

Career Connection: Reading about Job Requirements

1 MATCH the numbers of the jobs with the job duties.

1 Administrative assistant

2 Health care worker

3 Web designer

a. _2_ take care of patients

b. ____ answer the phone

c. ____ design web pages

d. ____ organize documents

e. ____ answer e-mails

f. ____ talk with doctors

g. ____ use the Internet

h. ____ fix computer problems

i. ____ explain medications

2 READ the sentences about the workers. Match the training courses with the workers to help them improve their job skills.

a Office Skills and Business Equipment	c Workplace Communication	e Time and Stress Management
b Telephone Skills	d ~~Records Management~~	f Written Business Communications

1. _d_ Lisa has trouble organizing papers and documents. She can never find anything in her office.

2. ____ Lisa doesn't understand how to use some of the office machines.

3. ____ Ling is often stressed and angry at work. She has too much work to do.

4. ____ Ling needs to talk with patients and doctors in a confident way. But he sometimes feels nervous.

5. ____ Ted needs to write business letters but he doesn't know the correct language for formal letters.

6. ____ Ted needs to talk on the phone with his customers in a friendly way.

3 WHAT job skills do you want to improve? What kind of training do you need?

I want to improve _____.

I need to study _____.

4 EDIT. The paragraph has six verb mistakes. Find them and correct them.

has

Leslie wants to be a fashion designer. She ~~have~~ three main goals for her career. Her first goal is to improve her English. She taking English classes right now in speaking and writing. She going to read and study about fashion. Her second goal is to study fashion at art school. In her free time, she make beautiful and interesting designs. She often use the Internet to find information about fashion. Her third goal is to work for a famous fashion designer in New York. She working hard to reach these goals.

Technology Connection: Searching a Library Catalog

You can search a library catalog in different ways.
- By key word. For example, to find information about choosing a career, type: *career advice*.
- By title. Type in the full title of the book.
- By author. Type in the last name of the author or the last name followed by the first name. For example: *Jones, Alan*
- By subject. For example, to learn about how to be a graphic designer, type: *graphic design*.

Library Catalog

Search By:
⦿ Keyword ○ Title ○ Author ○ Subject

Search for [＿＿＿＿] Limit to: [Books ▼] [Submit search]
                                       Journals
                                       Videos
                                       DVDs
                                       CDs

A READ the sentences. Complete the chart with the search information.
1. You want to find a book named *The Pearl*.
2. You want to find a book by John Steinbeck.
3. You want to find a DVD about famous places in the United States.
4. You want to find a CD by Enrique Iglesias.

Search by	Search for	Limit to
title	The Pearl	books

B REAL-LIFE LESSON.

1. Find your school's online library catalog, or find your local public library online.

   Write the website address: ＿＿＿＿＿＿＿＿＿＿＿＿＿＿＿＿＿＿＿＿＿

2. Search the catalog for books about English grammar.

   Write one book title: ＿＿＿＿＿＿＿＿＿＿＿＿＿＿＿＿＿＿＿＿＿

Practice Test

WCD, 6
🎧 **LISTENING:** Listen to the question. Then listen to the conversation. Listen to the question again. Choose the correct answer.

1. Ⓐ Ⓑ Ⓒ   2. Ⓐ Ⓑ Ⓒ

WCD, 7
🎧 **LISTENING:** Listen to the conversation. Then choose the correct answer.

3. What is Frank's priority this semester?
   A. He's going to be on time.
   B. He's going to do his homework.
   C. He's going to see a counselor.

4. What is Iva's problem?
   A. She is often absent.
   B. She's often late.
   C. She gets bad grades.

5. How is Frank going to get support?
   A. He's going to talk with the instructor.
   B. He's going to ask his family.
   C. He's going to see an academic counselor.

GRAMMAR: Choose the correct word or phrase to complete each sentence.

6. Jan with her academic counselor now.
   A. meet
   B. meets
   C. is meeting
   D. doesn't meet

9. _____ Max going to stick to a schedule?
   A. Is
   B. Are
   C. Do
   D. Did

8. Did Raffi _____ class every day last semester?
   A. attend
   B. attends
   C. attending
   D. attended

9. Sam and Jess usually _____ their homework in the library.
   A. do
   B. does
   C. is doing
   D. are doing

10. _____ Jung and Leo late for class yesterday?
    A. Did
    B. Is
    C. Are
    D. Were

VOCABULARY: Choose the best word or phrase to complete the sentence.

11. You can ask the _____ to help you with any problems on the computer.
    A. lab assistant
    B. counselor
    C. custodian
    D. receptionist

12. You can find books, magazines, CDs, and other kinds of _____ in the library.
    A. classes
    B. resources
    C. advice
    D. assignments

13. You can get advice about courses, careers, and jobs from your ____.
    A. lab assistant
    B. tutor
    C. librarian
    D. academic counselor

14. My family and friends helped me to study. They gave me a lot of ____.
    A. goals
    B. responsibility
    C. support
    D. attention

15. It is a good idea to plan your time and stick to a ____.
    A. goal
    B. support
    C. priority
    D. schedule

READING: Read Fernando's journal. Choose the correct answer.

<u>Learning new words</u> It's easy for me to remember new words if the teacher says them first. It's more difficult to read words from the book. I need to hear the words and then say them to a classmate. I borrow CDs from the library so I can practice the pronunciation.

<u>Learning grammar</u> I like to hear example sentences using the new grammar. Dictation is my favorite class activity. I sometimes read my assignments aloud. I need to hear the grammar many times to help me remember it.

16. This journal is about ____.
    A. one student's learning style
    B. different types of learning styles
    C. problems with learning
    D. advice about how to learn

17. Fernando writes about learning ____.
    A. grammar
    B. vocabulary
    C. grammar and vocabulary
    D. pronunciation

18. Fernando has a(n) ____ learning style.
    A. visual
    B. kinesthetic
    C. auditory
    D. varied

19. Which activity matches Fernando's learning style?
    A. Draw pictures of new words.
    B. Put study notes around your home.
    C. Work with a study group.
    D. Highlight new words in the textbook.

20. Which words in the journal help you identify Fernando's learning style?
    A. learn, remember
    B. hear, listen
    C. borrow, practice
    D. read, find

Lesson 1

1 **WRITE** the words for the products.

1
_____microwave_____

2
_____

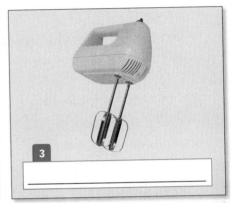

3
_____

4
_____

5
_____

6
_____

2 **COMPLETE** the sentences. Use adjectives to make comparisons about the microwaves.

Marina microwave	**Cresta** microwave
450 kW	450 kW
24 different settings	3 settings: low/medium/high
Size: large	Size: medium
Average energy use: 150 kWh per year	Average energy use: 200 kWh per year

1. The Marina microwave is _____*larger than*_____ (large) the Cresta.

2. The Cresta microwave is _____ (small) the Marina.

3. The Marina microwave is _____ (powerful) the Cresta.

4. The Cresta microwave is _____ (complicated) the Marina.

5. The Marina microwave is _____ (energy efficient) the Cresta.

Lesson 2

1 **COMPLETE** the chart. Use the words in the box. Then add two more items to each column.

armchair	DVD player	electric toothbrush	hair dryer
~~refrigerator~~	sofa	TV	vacuum cleaner

Household appliances	Furniture	Personal care
refrigerator		

2 **MATCH** the opposites. Write the letters.

1. __c__ attractive
2. _____ comfortable
3. _____ convenient
4. _____ heavy
5. _____ old-fashioned

a. light
b. modern
c. ~~ugly~~
d. inconvenient
e. uncomfortable

3 **COMPLETE** the questions. Use comparatives.

1. Which TV is _____more modern_____ (modern)?

2. Which vacuum cleaner is _____ (heavy)?

3. Which electric razor is _____ (good)?

4. Which DVD player is _____ (reliable)?

4 **COMPLETE** the sentences. Use comparatives with the same meaning.

1. The blue armchair is more comfortable than the red one.

   The red armchair is _less comfortable than the blue one._____

2. The silver hair dryer is more convenient than the black one.

   The black hair dryer is not _____.

3. The orange sofa and the green sofa are both attractive.

   The orange sofa is _____.

Lesson 3

1 LISTEN to the conversation. Then listen to the question. Fill in the circle for the correct answer.

WCD, 8

1. (A) (B) (C)
2. (A) (B) (C)
3. (A) (B) (C)

2 LISTEN. Then read the questions and choose the correct answer.

WCD, 9

1. Where are the speakers?

   A. at home

   B. in a restaurant

   C. in a store

2. Why does Bob prefer his microwave?

   A. It's more powerful.

   B. It uses less energy.

   C. The food tastes better.

3. Why does Amy prefer a conventional oven?

   A. It's easier to use.

   B. It's more convenient.

   C. It's different.

3 WRITE the lines of the conversation in the correct order.

Excuse me. How much are these hair dryers?
The larger one is more powerful, but it's heavier.
How about this model? It's not as expensive and it's lighter.
The small one is $25. The larger one is $50.
Thank you for your help. I'll think about it.
That's not so good. I need something lighter.
I see. Which one is more powerful?

A: _Excuse me. How much are these hair dryers?_____

B: _____

A: _____

B: _____

A: _____

B: _____

A: _____

4 PRACTICE the conversation in Activity 3 with a partner. Write a conversation about a different product in your notebook.

Culture and Communication: Class Participation

1 **READ** the student reports.

Student Reports		
	Emmy	**Kim**
Attendance	Good	Excellent
Homework	Very good	Fair
Motivation	Good	Good
Class participation	Weak	Excellent

2 **CHECK** ☑ *True* or *False*.

	True	False
1. Emmy's attendance is as good as Kim's.	☐	☐
2. Emmy's homework is better than Kim's.	☐	☐
3. Kim is as motivated as Emmy.	☐	☐
4. Emmy's class participation is not as good as Kim's.	☐	☐

3 **DISCUSS** with a partner. Which of the following do you think is included in the meaning of "class participation"?

- always attends class
- is always on time for class
- answers the teacher's questions
- asks the teacher questions
- cooperates with other students
- listens carefully
- talks actively in pair and group work
- takes notes

> **Culture Tip**
>
> In the United States, the teacher often gives a grade for "class participation." It is a good idea to find out from your teacher exactly what this means. It usually includes some of the following: *asking questions, talking actively in class, cooperating with others,* and *coming to class on time.*

4 **WRITE.**

1. Write your definition of excellent class participation. Compare the definition of class participation in the U.S. with your own country.

_____

_____

_____

2. How do you rate your class participation? Why?

   ☐ Weak   ☐ Fair   ☐ Good   ☐ Very Good   ☐ Excellent

_____

Lesson 4

1 COMPLETE the sentences. Use the adjectives in the box.

colorful	durable	good value	practical	stylish

1. It has lots of different colors in it. It's very _____ colorful _____.

2. You can wear them every day. They're _____.

3. Buy a pack of three and they're only $1 each. They're _____.

4. It's the latest fashion. It's very _____.

5. They're very strong. They will last a long time. They're _____.

2 READ the information about the backpacks. Complete the questions. Use superlatives. Then write short answers to the questions. Use *one* or *ones* to replace the noun.

1. Which backpack is _____ the heaviest _____ (heavy)? _____ The largest one. _____

2. Which backpack is _____ (colorful)? _____

3. Which backpack is _____ (cheap)? _____

4. Which backpack is _____ (expensive)? _____

5. Which backpack is _____ (good value)? _____

3 MATH. Calculate prices and savings. Circle the correct answer.

1. One sweater costs $30. The regular price is $40. You will save   **a.** $20.   **(b.** $10.)

2. Three T-shirts cost $12. Each T-shirt costs   **a.** $6.   **b.** $4.

3. One pair of boots costs $27.99. The regular price is $38. You will save   **a.** $10.01.   **b.** $9.99.

4. The suitcase costs $17.50. The regular price is $35. You will save   **a.** $35.   **b.** $17.50.

5. Three pairs of socks cost $9. Each pair costs   **a.** $3.   **b.** $4.

Lesson 5

1 **READ** about three refrigerators. Complete the sentences. Use *most, least,* or *–est*.

Refrigerator Comparison Chart		
Keepcool Refrigerator	**Extracool Refrigerator**	**Supercool Refrigerator**
Size 19 inches × 16 inches × 18 inches	66 inches × 33 inches × 30 inches	70 inches × 36 inches × 32 inches
Energy 200 watts per year	700 watts per year	600 watts per year
Price $175	$750	$960

1. The Supercool refrigerator is _____*the largest*_____ (large)

2. The Keepcool refrigerator is _____ (small).

3. The Keepcool refrigerator is _____ (energy efficient).

4. The Extracool refrigerator is _____ (energy efficient).

5. The Keepcool refrigerator is _____ (expensive).

6. The Supercool refrigerator is _____ (expensive).

2 **USE YOUR DICTIONARY.** Write the opposites of the adjectives in the box.

attractive	comfortable	complicated	convenient	efficient	~~expensive~~	reliable

in-	*un-*
inexpensive	

3 **WRITE** the answers to the riddles. Unscramble the names of these electrical appliances.

1. It's usually in the kitchen. It's bigger than a toaster, but it's smaller than a stove.

   It's a _____. **cromvewia**

2. It's usually in the kitchen. It's more complicated than a toaster. It's smaller than a dishwasher.
   It's a _____. **cramoferfeke**

3. It's usually in the bathroom or bedroom. It's heavier than a toothbrush. It's not as complicated as a
   camera. It's a _____ _____. **ryahirder**

4. It's usually in the living room or the bedroom. It's bigger than a CD player. It's less expensive than a
   TV. It's a _____ _____. **ylperdavd**

Family Connection: Choosing the Best Payment Method

1 **TALK** with a partner. Discuss the questions about paying bills.

How does your family usually pay the bills for gas, electricity, water, and phone? Are they paid all in the same way? Who usually pays the bills? Does your family have a system for paying and recording bill payments?

2 **READ** the information about payment options. How many payment methods are there? Check ☑ the options you usually use.

Utility Bill Payment Options	
☐ **By check**	Mail your check to: Finance Department 400 South Street PO Box 1234 Chicago, IL 60610
☐ **By phone**	Pay bills by phone at (630) 555-9808 using a debit or credit card during normal business hours.
☐ **Online**	Access your account online and pay by debit or credit card any time.
☐ **Direct debit**	Payments are taken automatically from your bank account.

3 **WRITE.** What are the advantages and disadvantages of each payment method in Activity 2? Which one is cheaper, safer, easier, or faster? Complete the chart. Which one is the best for your family?

	Advantages	Disadvantages
By check	You can keep a paper record of each bill and payment.	
By phone		
Online		
Direct debit		

4 **READ** the article. Then match each banking term with its description. Write the letters.

Which is better, a debit card or a credit card?

What is the difference between a debit card and a credit card? You can use both of them in stores or to pay over the phone or online A debit card looks like a credit card, but it works more like cash or a personal check. With a debit card, you pay now. With a credit card, you pay later.

Bob uses his debit card for almost all his purchases. He says it is more convenient than cash and he doesn't have a huge bill to pay at the end of the month. Debit cards work like cash or a personal check. The money is automatically taken out of your bank account. But be careful! If someone steals your debit card, it's easy for them to get all the money in your account.

Sandy uses a credit card for all her bills and payments. She says it is easier to pay just one bill at the end of each month. Sometimes she doesn't have enough money in her account and she pays it off the next month. When you use a credit card, you are borrowing money. You have to pay back the money each month. But be careful! If you pay back less than the full amount, you have to pay interest.

1. __d__ debit card   a. place where you can put your money

2. _____ credit card   b. ask someone to lend you money (for a short time)

3. _____ account   c. the cost of borrowing money

4. _____ borrow   d. ~~you can use this to get money from your account~~

5. _____ interest   e. you can use this to borrow money

5 **READ** the article again. Answer the questions.

1. What is one advantage of a debit card? What is one disadvantage?

_____

2. What is one advantage of a credit card? What is one disadvantage?

_____

6 **REAL-LIFE LESSON.** What kind of credit card(s) do you have? Why is it better (or worse) than other credit cards? Why did you choose it? Discuss with a partner.

Community Connection: Choosing a Computer for Your Community Center

1 **READ** the computer information in the chart. Then answer the questions. Write the numbers.

	1	2	3
Price/Value Rating Key: ◼◼◼◼ Excellent / ◼◼◼☐ Very Good / ◼◼☐☐ Good / ◼☐☐☐ Poor			
Price	$479	$399	$695
Price/Value Rating	◼◼◼◼	◼◼☐☐	◼◼◼☐
Memory (RAM)	512	512	256
Graphics Card (RAM)	256	128	64
Mouse	✓	✓	✗
Parts and Labor Warranty	1 year	3 years	1 year
Phone Support	1 year	3 months	None
E-mail Support	None	1 year	3 months

1. Which computer is the largest? __2__

2. Which computer is the most expensive? _____

3. Which computer is the most convenient for travel? _____

4. Which computer is the most powerful? _____

5. Which computer has the longest warranty? _____

2 **TALK** in a group. Which computer is best for a community center? Why? Tell your reasons to the class.

3 COMPLETE the missing parts of the complaint letter. Use the words in the box.

bill	company	faster	computer	repair	~~Sir~~	truly	warranty

Glenview Community Center • South Creek, NC 28250

Texas Computer Co.
6590 Western Road
Houston, TX 77002

December 21, 2008

Dear ___Sir___ or Madam,

   I purchased a _____ for our community center from your

_____ on December 12, 2008. It cost $399. At first, we were very

pleased because it was _____ than our old computer, but now there is

a problem. It makes a strange clicking sound. I have a one-year _____.

Could you please _____ my computer or replace it as soon as possible?

I am enclosing a copy of my _____ and my warranty.

Yours _____,

Janice Higgins

Janice Higgins
Community Center Treasurer

4 WRITE. You recently bought a microwave oven for your community center from the Microwave Oven Company at 65001 Forkbend Road, Houston, TX, 77020. The oven was larger and more powerful than your old microwave. But it makes a strange buzzing sound and it beeps all the time. Write a letter of complaint.

5 REAL-LIFE LESSON. Find out about warranties on products in your local store. Choose one product. How long is the warranty? What does it cover? Can you get a refund?

Career Connection: Comparing Jobs

1 **MATCH** the pictures with the jobs. Write the names of the jobs.

accountant	administrative assistant	nurse	engineer

1. _____

2. _____

3. _____

4. _____

2 **READ** the descriptions. Match the descriptions with the jobs in Activity 1. Write the numbers of the jobs.

1. _____ I work with sick people and help them to get better. I work in a hospital and I sometimes go to people's homes. I help people take care of themselves. I need to know what to do in a medical emergency. Sometimes it is stressful.

2. _____ I need good computer skills for this job. It helps to speak more than one language. I spend a lot of time answering e-mail and answering the phone. I also make appointments and travel arrangements. For this job, I need to be organized, well dressed, polite, and friendly.

3. _____ I track all the company's profits and expenses. I need to use computer programs to calculate costs and profits. I need to understand tax rules and government rules for keeping records. For this job, I need to be careful and have good math skills.

4. _____ I design buildings, highways, bridges, airports, and railroads. I need to know how to plan and manage projects, how to calculate costs, and how to buy equipment and materials. I need to understand how to make buildings safe. For this job, I need to work well with other people in a team.

3 **COMPLETE** the chart. Check ☑ which of these jobs you find most interesting, creative, dangerous, or stressful. Tell a partner why.

	Accountant	Administrative Assistant	Engineer	Nurse
Interesting				✓
Creative				
Dangerous				
Stressful				

Example: *I think the nurse's job is the most interesting because you can learn a lot about health and medicine.*

4 EDIT. Five words are missing in the paragraph. Use the words in the box.

a	I	is	more	~~to~~

My Dream Job

           ^{to}
I want find job as a TV journalist. I like to interview people. I want to film true stories about ordinary people. I think this job is interesting than an office worker in a large company. It also more dangerous. Maybe can get a higher salary, too. Maybe I can try to help solve problems and make life better for some people.

5 WRITE a paragraph. Describe a job that you do or want to do. Why is it better (or more interesting) than other jobs?

💻 **Technology Connection:** Using a Comparison Website

A comparison website compares different products. It helps you decide which product is best for you.

A THINK ABOUT IT. Think of an item you would like to buy such as a digital camera or a refrigerator. What do you want to compare about the product?

B INTERNET SEARCH. Go on the Internet. Find comparison websites for three different types or brands of the item. Type in the keyword *comparison* and the name of your product, such as *digital camera*. Write the Web addresses here. What does the website compare for each product? (price, size)

1. Type of product _____ website _____

   This website compares _____

2. Type of product _____ website _____

   This website compares _____

3. Type of product _____ website _____

   This website compares _____

Practice Test

LISTENING: Listen to the conversation. Then listen to the question. Choose the correct answer.

1. (A) (B) (C)   2. (A) (B) (C)

LISTENING: Listen to the conversation. Then choose the correct answer.

3. What does the speaker want to buy?
   A. a T-shirt
   B. a sweater
   C. a sweatshirt

4. What's wrong with the blue one?
   A. It's the most stylish one.
   B. It's the most expensive one.
   C. It's the least attractive one.

5. Which does the speaker decide to buy?
   A. the most practical one
   B. the cheapest one
   C. the most colorful one

GRAMMAR: Choose the correct word or phrase to complete each sentence.

6. The large mixer is ____ the small one.
   A. the less complicated than
   B. less complicated as
   C. less complicated than
   D. more complicated as

7. The small microwave is ____ as the large one.
   A. not as expensive
   B. more expensive
   C. not expensive
   D. less expensive

8. The large suitcase is ____ as the small one.
   A. lighter
   B. as light
   C. more heavier
   D. the least heavy

9. Which is ____, a dishwasher or a washing machine?
   A. the least expensive
   B. more expensive
   C. the less expensive
   D. the more expensive

10. Which boots are the best value? ____.
    A. The brown ones.
    B. The brown one.
    C. The brown.
    D. Brown ones.

VOCABULARY: Choose the best word or phrase to complete the sentence.

11. The dishwasher is not easy to use. It's very ____.
    A. complicated
    B. powerful
    C. convenient
    D. reliable

12. This air conditioner uses a lot of electricity. It's not ____.
    A. reliable
    B. powerful
    C. convenient
    D. energy efficient

13. You can find a vacuum cleaner in the ____ section of a store.
    A. household appliances
    B. furniture
    C. personal care
    D. electronics

14. The blue suitcase is the strongest. It's very ____.
    A. stylish
    B. durable
    C. good value
    D. colorful

15. You can wear this coat in all types of weather. It's very ____.
    A. stylish
    B. good value
    C. practical
    D. comfortable

READING: Read. Choose the correct answer.

Phone or e-mail: Which do you like better?

Lily: I like talking on the phone better than e-mail. It's less complicated than e-mail. I don't need to think about spelling or grammar. I sometimes spend hours on the phone talking with my friends. I think it's more personal and it's easier to express my feelings.

Pran: E-mails are easier and faster. You can think about what to say and you can say it more clearly. They're more convenient because you can send an e-mail to friends at work, for example, and it doesn't disturb them. They can answer you later. You can keep e-mails and read them again later. E-mail is faster than a phone call. It's more useful at work if you are very busy.

---

16. Which one is true?
    A. Both writers prefer phone calls.
    B. Both writers prefer e-mail.
    C. One writer prefers phone calls.
    D. Both writers dislike e-mail.

17. Lily prefers phone calls because ____.
    A. they're easier
    B. they're faster
    C. they save time
    D. they're less expensive

18. Pran prefers e-mails because ____.
    A. they're more personal
    B. they're easier
    C. they save time
    D. they're less expensive

19. Why does Lily think phone calls are more personal?
    A. You can express your feelings.
    B. It's less complicated.
    C. You can check your grammar.
    D. You can answer any time.

20. Why does Pran think e-mail is more convenient?
    A. You can express your feelings.
    B. You can think about what to say.
    C. You can check your grammar.
    D. You can answer any time.

Lesson 1

1 **MATCH** the pictures and the phrases. Write the letters.

1

2

3

4

5

6

a. changing lanes	c. sitting in a car seat	e. talking on a cell phone
b. ~~speeding~~	d. driving alone in a carpool lane	f. parking in a handicapped parking space

2 **COMPLETE** the sentences. Write the simple past or past continuous form of the verb.

1. Tony _____*was speeding*_____ (speed) when the police officer _____ (see) him.

2. I _____ (not, use) my turn signal when I _____ (turn) the corner.

3. Jess _____ (not, pay) attention when she _____ (change) lanes.

4. When the accident _____ (happen), Tim _____ (sit) in a car seat.

5. You _____ (talk) on your cell phone when you _____ (hit) my car.

6. When the police officer _____ (stop) them, Tom and Lisa _____

   (drive) in a carpool lane.

Lesson 2

1 COMPLETE the questions. Write the past continuous form of the verb.

1. What _____*was he doing*_____ (he / do) at 10 A.M.?

2. Where _____ (Dan / park)?

3. Who _____ (not, sit) in a car seat?

4. Where _____ (Tran and Luis / drive)?

5. Who _____ (not, wearing) a helmet?

6. Why _____ (Tina / hitchhiking)?

7. Who _____ (sleep) in the car?

8. Who _____ (you, talk) to on your cell phone?

2 MATCH the questions with the answers. Write the letters.

__c__ 1. What were Sara and Jon doing?

_____ 2. Where was Sue parking?

_____ 3. Where were you going?

_____ 4. Who was riding a bike?

_____ 5. What was Bob doing?

_____ 6. What was Tim wearing?

a. He was passing another car.

b. A bike helmet.

c. ~~They were driving to work.~~

d. In a parking space.

e. To the hospital.

f. Matt.

3 MATH. Solve the problems. Use numbers and *miles under/over.*

1. Todd was driving 45 miles an hour in a 35-mile-per-hour zone.
   He was driving _____*10 miles over*_____ the speed limit!

2. Martina was driving 10 miles an hour in a 25-mile-per-hour zone.
   She was driving _____ the speed limit.

3. Nassim was driving 65 miles an hour in a 60-mile-per-hour zone.
   He was driving _____ the speed limit.

4. Jasmin was driving 25 miles an hour in a 45-mile-per-hour zone.
   She was driving _____ the speed limit.

Lesson 3

1 **LISTEN.** Write the numbers under the pictures.

a

b

c

_____   _____   _____

2 **LISTEN** to the question. Then listen to the conversation. Listen to the question again. Fill in the circle for the correct answer.

1. Ⓐ Ⓑ Ⓒ
2. Ⓐ Ⓑ Ⓒ
3. Ⓐ Ⓑ Ⓒ

3 **WRITE** the lines of the conversation in the correct order.

Angela? You were late for class this morning.

Oh, no! Was he hurt?

I'm sorry. I had a family emergency.

I'm glad to hear that.

My son was riding his bike to school when he hit a tree and fell.

No, not badly. He's fine.

I hope it wasn't serious. What happened?

A: _Angela? You were late for class this morning._

B: _____

A: _____

B: _____

A: _____

B: _____

A: _____

4 **PRACTICE** the conversation with a partner.

Culture and Communication: Making Excuses for Being Late

1 READ. Some students were late for class this morning. Which of these excuses do you think are good? Rate them on a scale of 1 to 3. 1 = good, 2 = okay, 3 = not good. Compare your answers with a partner and your teacher.

Excuse (reason for being late)	Rating		
I didn't get up on time.	①	②	③
I was finishing my homework.	①	②	③
My bus was late.	①	②	③
I was getting a book from the library.	①	②	③
I had a car accident.	①	②	③
I missed my bus.	①	②	③
My son was sick.	①	②	③

Culture Tip

U.S. culture places great importance on being on time at school or at work. Good excuses for being late are usually serious health or family issues.

2 MATCH the excuses with the response from the teacher. Write the letters.

_____e____ 1. I was talking to a friend.

_____ 2. I was getting a book from the library.

_____ 3. I had a car accident.

_____ 4. My bus was late.

_____ 5. My son was sick.

_____ 6. I didn't get up on time.

a. That's terrible. Are you okay?

b. Yes, my bus is often late, too.

c. Do you need a better alarm clock?

d. I'm so sorry. I hope he feels better.

e. ~~It's important to be on time for class.~~

f. Why don't you go there after class?

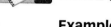

3 WRITE a conversation. Use sentences from Activity 2.

Example:

Student: I'm sorry I was late this morning.

Teacher: What happened?

Student: I was talking to a friend and I lost track of the time.

Teacher: It's important to be on time for class, you know. Please try to arrive on time in the future.

Student: Yes, I will.

4 PRACTICE your conversation with a partner.

Lesson 4

1 **COMPLETE** the sentences. Use the simple past of the verbs in the box.

bump	burn	~~cut~~	fall off	sprain	trip

1 She ___cut___ her hand.

2 She _____ her wrist.

3 He _____ over a rope.

4 He _____ his head.

5 He _____ his hand.

6 She _____ the swing.

2 **MATCH** the sentence parts. Write the letters.

___b___ **1.** I hurt my head

_____ **2.** I burned my hand

_____ **3.** I dislocated my shoulder

_____ **4.** I sprained my ankle

_____ **5.** I tripped on the carpet

_____ **6.** I cut my finger

a. while I was lifting furniture.

b. ~~while I was playing football.~~

c. while I was jogging.

d. while I was cooking.

e. while I was opening a can.

f. while I was climbing the stairs.

3 **UNDERLINE** the correct verb forms.

1. While Janice *worked* / *was working* in the garden, she *hurt* / *was hurting* her hand.

2. Gary *dislocated* / *was dislocating* his wrist while he *moved* / *was moving* some tables.

3. While Tamara *rode* / *was riding* a bike, she *fell* / *was falling* off and hurt her arm.

4. Leon and Hassan *burned* / *were burning* their fingers while they *cooked* / *were cooking*.

5. Pia and Francisco *hurt* / *were hurting* their backs while they *cleaned* / *were cleaning* the floor.

6. While they *left* / *were leaving* the building, Tony and Minh *slipped* / *were slipping* on the stairs.

Lesson 5

1 **USE YOUR DICTIONARY.** Use the words in the box to answer the questions.

lift	sprain	happen	dislocate	break	work	trip	bump	cut

1. Which verbs are irregular in the simple past?

   _____

2. Which verbs have more than one syllable?

   _____

3. Which verbs describe accidents or injuries?

   _____

4. Which verbs have two vowels together? Practice the pronunciation with a partner.

   _____

5. Write the verbs in alphabetical order.

   _____

   _____

2 **COMPLETE** the sentences to find the answers to the crossword puzzle.

Across

1. While she was taking pizza out of the oven, Dana _____ her hand.

2. Dan _____ over a stone while he was running for the bus.

3. Bob _____ his shoulder while he was lifting some boxes.

4. Maria _____ off the swing while playing in the park.

Down

5. While Larry was playing tennis, he _____ his ankle.

6. Linda _____ on the ice while she was walking to school.

7. I hurt my finger while I was playing baseball, but I didn't _____ it.

8. While Carmen was getting out of the car, she _____ her head.

B U R N E D

Family Connection: Child Safety

1 WRITE. Label each of these traffic safety items.

| bicycle helmet | booster seat | ~~car seat~~ | reflective clothing | seat belt |

_____   _____   _____   _____   _____

2 COMPLETE the sentences with words from Activity 1.

1. Infants must sit in a _____car seat_____ when they are in a car.

2. Older children must sit in a _____.

3. Everyone in a car must wear a _____.

4. If you ride a bicycle at night, you should wear _____.

5. To prevent a head injury, you should wear a _____.

3 WRITE. A police officer stopped Jimmy at 6:00 P.M. last night. What was Jimmy doing wrong?

1. He _____was talking on a cell phone._____

2. He _____

3. He _____

4. He _____

4 REAL-LIFE LESSON.

1. Go online and search for information about traffic safety for children. Find three useful tips for helping your children travel safely: in a car, on a bike, or when they are walking near traffic.

2. Find three websites that can give you information about child car seat safety. Find out if your child's car seat or booster seat meets safety standards.

5 **READ** about Jimmy. Complete the chart.

Jimmy was riding his bike near his home on Friday night. It was already dark, and he was late for dinner. He was turning the corner of his street and calling his parents on his cell phone when he hit a tree and fell off his bike. A police officer was driving by and helped Jimmy get home. He also gave Jimmy some advice about traffic safety.

Wh- question chart	
Who (Who had the accident?)	*Jimmy*
What (What happened?)	
Where (Where did the accident happen?)	
When (When did the accident happen?)	
Why / How (Why or how did the accident happen?)	

6 **MATCH.** Joe and Shula were driving home with their children. Match the questions with the answers.

1. Who?
2. What?
3. Where?
4. When?
5. Why/How?

a. One child was not wearing a seat belt. One child was not sitting in a car seat.

b. In front of their home

c. Joe and Shula and their children

d. Friday night

e. Joe's car hit a parked car while he was parking. The children hit their heads against the window.

7 **WRITE** a paragraph describing Joe and Shula's accident.

Joe and Shula were driving home with their children on Friday night. Joe was parking the car in

front of their home when _____

_____

_____

_____

_____

Community Connection: Traffic Safety in Your Neighborhood

1 READ. Scan the flyer. Match the headings with the pictures. Write the letters.

 Community Action Group: *Making Our Neighborhood Safer*

Dear Neighbors,

Are you worried about your children's safety? There are more cars in our streets every day. It's not as safe for our children to walk and play. Join our neighborhood community action group and help to make our neighborhood safer. Here are some of the suggestions we want to discuss at our meeting.

1. Crosswalks _d_

Cars don't stop for pedestrians. It's difficult to cross the street, and people sometimes have to wait a long time. We need more crosswalks.

2. Speed Bumps _____

Do cars drive over the speed limit down your street? Speed bumps can slow cars down to about 15 mph.

3. Speed Radar Signs _____

Speed radar signs can record the speed of passing cars. Drivers can see their speed on the sign. The police can send police officers to stop speeding.

4. Bicycle Lanes _____

More bicycle lanes on busy streets will make the streets safer for bike riders. You and your children can ride your bikes more safely.

5. Safety Signs _____

Safety signs can warn drivers that children are in the area. We aren't sure if they help and we'd like to hear your opinion.

Join our neighborhood community action group and help us make our neighborhood streets safer. Attend the next community action group meeting. Your voice counts!

2 MATCH. Which paragraph in Activity 1 goes with each problem below? Write the numbers.

_2_ Drivers were driving too fast down our street.

_____ Cars didn't give space to bicycles.

_____ Cars were not stopping for pedestrians.

_____ Drivers weren't paying attention to their speed.

_____ Drivers weren't watching out for children.

3 FIND AND MATCH. Find the words in the flyer on page 42. Then match the words with their meanings.

1. _____ a crosswalk

2. _____ a pedestrian

3. _____ a bicycle lane

4. _____ speed bumps

a. a person who is walking

b. bumps on the roads that help to slow down drivers

c. a part of the road only for bicycles

d. a place where you can cross the street; white lines are painted on the street to help drivers see pedestrians

4 READ the article. Then answer the questions.

Speed Radar gets a "YES!"

Residents of Willow Street, South Town were happy to hear that the city council agreed to a speed radar sign on their street at the city council meeting last Thursday. "We're very pleased," said Shirlee Johnson. "Cars were driving down our street way over the speed limit." "My son was riding his bike on the sidewalk last year when a speeding car almost hit him," said Sam Forrester, another Willow Street resident. "Now I hope they'll keep to the speed limit."

1. What was the problem on Willow Street?

_____

2. What happened to one resident's son?

_____

3. What are they going to do about the problem?

_____

5 REAL-LIFE LESSON. Think of a problem with safety in your neighborhood. What could you do about the problem? Write problems and the solutions in your notebook.

Example:

Problem	Solution
Our children sometimes play in the street outside our homes. People drive too fast down the street.	We could ask the city council to put up a speed radar sign. It could help to slow down cars in our neighborhood.

Career Connection: Read a Work Accident Report

1 **READ** the paragraph.

Brief Description of the Accident:

The employee is a truck driver with three years of experience in this position. He is 45 years old. The accident happened while he was moving some boxes from his truck to the delivery area. The employee was taking the boxes out of his truck when he fell and hurt his arm. Another truck driver was working in the same area, and he saw the accident. He informed the manager, and the manager drove the employee to the hospital.

2 **COMPLETE** the accident report. Use the information in Activity 1. Draw a picture of the accident.

EMPLOYEE ACCIDENT REPORT

Summary No. 48

Date of accident: _September 16_   **Date report filed:** _September 17_

Location of accident:		
Accident type:		
Type of injury:		
Employee job title:		
Age:		
Sex:		
Length of time in position:		

3 **COMPLETE** the chart with names of other jobs. What other types of accidents can happen at work?

Type of job	Type of accident

4 EDIT. The paragraph has six mistakes. Find them and correct them.

The accident happen *ed* while I was cooking some pancakes for my family. I put some oil into the pan and turned on the gas. Then my daughter asked me for some fruit. While I getting fruit for my daughter, I forgot about the pan. When I came back to the stove, the pan was burn and there was a lot of smoke. I turned off the gas. When I try to pick up the pan and I burned my hand. I immediately was put my hand under cold water.

Technology Connection: Searching the Web

A READ the information about website addresses.

You can get information about a website by looking at the last three letters of the Web address. This can help you decide if the information is reliable.

- Government websites usually end in *.gov*. For example, *www.whitehouse.gov* is the Web address for the White House.

- University websites usually end in *.edu*. For example, *www.uoregon.edu* is the website of the University of Oregon. These websites have information about the university or college, but students also use these websites to present their own information.

- Many non-profit organizations (including religious and political organizations) use the ending *.org*. For example, *www.ipl.org* is the website for the Internet Public Library.

- Most businesses and companies have websites ending in *.com*, *.net*, or *.biz*. These include news websites such as *www.cnn.com*.

B REAL-LIFE LESSON.

1. Does your school or college have a website?

   Write the address: _____

2. Find an English dictionary online.

   Write the address: _____

3. Find a government website that gives information about safety and health.

   Write the address: _____

Practice Test

WCD, 14 **LISTENING:** Listen to the question. Then listen to the conversation. Listen to the question again. Choose the correct answer.

1. Ⓐ   Ⓑ   Ⓒ   2. Ⓐ   Ⓑ   Ⓒ

WCD, 15 **LISTENING:** Listen to the conversation. Then choose the correct answer.

3. What happened to Harry?
   A. He bumped his head.
   B. He burned his wrist.
   C. He sprained his ankle.

4. What was he doing when the accident happened?
   A. He was climbing the stairs.
   B. He was running.
   C. He was playing football.

5. What is he going to do?
   A. He is going to the doctor.
   B. He is going to stay home.
   C. He is coming back to work tomorrow.

GRAMMAR: Choose the correct word or phrase to complete each sentence.

I wasn't (6) _____ a seat belt when the police officer (7) _____ me.

6. A. wear
   B. wears
   C. wore
   D. wearing

7. A. was stop
   B. was stopping
   C. stopped
   D. to stop

Sam (8) _____ his hand while he (9) _____.

8. A. was burn
   B. was burning
   C. was burned
   D. burned

9. A. was cook
   B. was cooking
   C. was cooked
   D. cooked

10. A: What was he doing when the police officer saw him?
    B: _____
    A. He was changing lanes.
    B. He stopped.
    C. He is driving.
    D. He wasn't wearing a seat belt.

VOCABULARY: Choose the best word or phrase to complete the sentence.

11. Paolo's driving over the speed limit. He's _____.
    A. parking
    B. changing lanes
    C. speeding
    D. passing

12. Leila's baby is in the car. The baby should sit in a _____.
    A. car seat
    B. seat belt
    C. front seat
    D. carpool lane

13. Tony's riding a bike. He should wear a _____.
   A. seat belt
   B. helmet
   C. headset
   D. cell phone

14. Sasha _____ on the wet floor and hurt her back.
   A. dislocated
   B. slipped
   C. sprained
   D. walked

15. I fell off my bike and I _____ my head.
   A. tripped
   B. bumped
   C. broke
   D. burned

READING: Read. Choose the correct answer.

> **Brief Description of the Accident**
>
> Patricia Jones is an office assistant with one and a half years of experience in this position. She is 25 years old. The accident happened while she was working in her office. The employee was standing up when she hit her head on a shelf. Another office assistant was working in the same office, and he saw the accident. He informed the manager, and she called an ambulance.

16. This report is about _____.
   A. a job
   B. an office
   C. an accident
   D. a manager

17. What happened to Patricia?
   A. She is 25 years old.
   B. She was working in her office.
   C. She was standing up.
   D. She hit her head.

18. What was she doing when the accident happened?
   A. She was standing up.
   B. She was going home.
   C. She was sitting down.
   D. She was talking to the manager.

19. What did the other office assistant do?
   A. He took Patricia home.
   B. He informed the manager.
   C. He called a doctor.
   D. He called an ambulance.

20. What did the manager do?
   A. She took Patricia home
   B. She called another office assistant
   C. She called a doctor
   D. She called an ambulance

UNIT 4 Laws, Rules, and Regulations

Lesson 1

1 COMPLETE the sentences. Use the words in the box.

| chatting | flip-flops | free meal | iPod® | ~~personal call~~ | shifts |

1 She's making a
personal call.

2 She's wearing
_____.

3 He's listening to an
_____.

4 They're _____.

5 He's eating a
_____.

6 They're exchanging
_____.

2 COMPLETE the sentences. Use *may, may not, can,* or *can't.*

1. Employees ___*may*___ have one free meal at work.

2. Employees _____ chat during the coffee break, but not while they are working.

3. _____ we make personal calls in the office?

4. We _____ exchange shifts with our coworkers, but we can ask the manager for a different shift.

5. Employees _____ wear flip-flops to work, but they may wear sandals.

6. We _____ listen to our iPods® while we're working, but we can listen during lunch.

3 WRITE three rules for your workplace or school. Use *may* or *may not.*

Example: *Students may not use their cell phones in class.*

1. _____

2. _____

3. _____

48 | Unit 4

Lesson 2

1 **COMPLETE** the conversation with *may, may not, can,* or *can't.*

It is Lisa's first day in her new job. A coworker is explaining the company rules.

Jen: The company rules are in the handbook. For example, in this section on the dress code,

it says "Company employees (1) ___may not___ wear jeans or sandals."

Lisa: Is that true? We can't wear jeans?

Jen: Well, it's usually true. Except for casual Fridays. Then we (2) _____ wear jeans and

sandals. But we (3) _____ wear sneakers.

Lisa: I see. What other rules are there?

Jen: There are rules about using the Internet. We (4) _____ surf the Internet and we

(5) _____ send personal e-mails during work hours.

Lisa: (6) _____ we send e-mails during our lunch break?

Jen: Yes, that's okay.

Lisa: What about phone calls? (7) _____ we make personal calls?

Jen: It's prohibited. Look at this page. It says "Employees (8) _____ make personal calls."

But you (9) _____ use your cell phone during the break. Look, here it says, "Employees

(10) _____ use cell phones or listen to iPods during work hours."

2 **WRITE** three questions to ask your boss or teacher about rules in your workplace or school.

Example: ___Can we wear sneakers to work (school)?___

1. _____

2. _____

3. _____

Lesson 3

1 **LISTEN** to the beginning of a conversation. Then listen for the next best sentence. Fill in the circle for the correct answer.

1. Ⓐ Ⓑ Ⓒ
2. Ⓐ Ⓑ Ⓒ
3. Ⓐ Ⓑ Ⓒ

2 **LISTEN** to the conversation. Circle the correct answer.

1. Why does Sara want to check the handbook?
   A. She wants to leave work early.
   B. She wants to take a break.
   C. She wants to go to the doctor.

2. How long is their normal lunch break?
   A. one hour
   B. 30 minutes
   C. 20 minutes

3. What time does Sara usually leave work?
   A. 5:30
   B. 6:00
   C. 7:00

3 **WRITE.** Number the lines of the conversation in the correct order.

_____ It says that we can't wear T-shirts to work.

_1_ Jim, do you know about the company dress code?

_____ Oh, I didn't know. You mean we can't wear short sleeves?

_____ Oh, I see. Thanks for telling me.

_____ We can wear short-sleeve shirts, but no T-shirts.

_____ A dress code? What's that?

4 **TALK** with a partner. Make a conversation about a rule at work or at school.

Culture and Communication: Classroom Rules

Culture Tip
Classroom rules in the United States can vary depending on the school and the teacher. It is not usually allowed to use cell phones, chew gum, or eat food during class. It is not polite to talk while the teacher is speaking. It is prohibited to copy work from another student's homework or during a test.

1 **WRITE** rules for your classroom. Use *may* or *may not*.

1. students / use cell phones

   Students may not use cell phones.

2. students / eat lunch in class

   _____

3. students / bring bottles of water, but no hot drinks

   _____

4. students / ask the teacher questions

   _____

5. students / enter the classroom late

   _____

6. students / copy homework

   _____

2 A new student is asking about classroom rules. Read the conversation.

Kim: Bill, can we bring a cell phone to class?

Bill: You can bring it to class, but you have to switch it off during the lesson.

Kim: You mean we can't answer any calls?

Bill: That's right. It gets too noisy and we can't hear the teacher.

Kim: Oh, I see. That sounds like a good reason.

3 **TALK** with a partner. Make a conversation about the rules in your classroom, or use the information in Activity 1. Give reasons for the rules.

Lesson 4

1 MATCH the rules with the items. Write the letters.

1. You must not smoke in ___c___
2. You must not run or shout in _____
3. You must park in your _____
4. You must put your garbage in _____
5. You must keep your dog on _____
6. You must not leave clothing in _____

a. the laundry room.
b. the Dumpster.
~~c. the common areas.~~
d. a leash.
e. the stairwell.
f. assigned space.

2 COMPLETE the sentences. <u>Underline</u> the correct words.

1. You *may not* / *have to* smoke in the building.
2. You *may* / *have to* be quiet in the hallway.
3. You *may not* / *have to* leave trash in the stairwell.
4. You *may not* / *have to* keep the common areas clear.
5. Residents *may* / *have to* park in the assigned spaces.
6. Visitors *may not* / *have to* park in the assigned spaces.

3 WRITE two rules for each place. Use the words in the box.

| ~~buy a ticket~~ | ride a bicycle | use your cell phone |
| check large bags | touch the pictures | walk on the grass |

1. You have to _buy a ticket._ _____

   You must not _____

2. You may _____

   You must not _____

3. You have to _____

   You must not _____

Lesson 5

1 MATH. Read the information. Calculate the expenses for Jerry and Beth.

1. Jerry wanted to go camping for one night. He booked a campsite in the national park for $20. He bought some firewood to build a fire. It cost $15. He borrowed a tent from his friend and a sleeping bag from his brother. He drove to the campsite and paid $20 to enter the park. He paid $25 for gas. How much did his camping trip cost?

campsite	$
firewood	$
entry fee	$
gas	$
Total	$

2. Beth wanted to go to a museum with her two friends. They went together in Beth's car. They paid $6 for the gas. They paid $9 to park the car in the museum garage. The entry fee was $10 for each person, but they got a group ticket for $18. How much did their trip cost for each person?

gas	$
parking	$
entry fee	$
Total	$
divide by 3 **Total per person**	$

2 USE YOUR DICTIONARY. Make nouns from these verbs. Which ending is different?

Verb	Noun
camp	*camper*
hike	
hunt	
ride	
swim	
visit	

3 READ the clues. Complete the puzzle. Unscramble the words. What is the mystery word?

1. Most companies have a _____ _____.   **scrosdeed**

2. Residents must put garbage in a _____.   **strudpem**

3. Employees may not wear _____.   **plopliffs**

4. You must keep your dog on a _____.   **helsa**

5. Park your car in the _____ space only.   **dinsesag**

1. __ ☐ __ __ __ __ __ __ __

2. __ ☐ __ __ __ __ __ __

3. __ ☐ __ __ __ __ __ __

4. __ ☐ __ __ __

5. __ ☐ __ __ __ __ __ __

Family Connection: After a Car Accident

1 **TALK** with a partner. Have you or a family member ever been in a car accident? Describe what happened.

2 **CHECK** ☑ the correct column for each action after a car accident. What do you have to do? What don't you have to do?

Action	Have to	Don't have to
call the police	☐	☑
call an ambulance	☐	☐
check to see if anyone is hurt	☐	☐
check damage to your car	☐	☐
say you're sorry	☐	☐
explain the reason for the accident	☐	☐
call your insurance company	☐	☐
exchange names with the other driver	☐	☐

3 **READ.** Then choose the best action for each situation.

1. Pete was backing his car out of a parking space in a busy parking lot behind the supermarket. A woman bicyclist rode behind his car. He didn't see her. He hit the bicyclist. The bicyclist fell to the ground. What should Pete do first?

   A. Check to see if the woman is hurt.
   B. Check damage to his car.
   C. Call an ambulance.

2. Brad was driving along a busy four-lane road. He stopped at a red light. The light turned green. The car next to him changed into his lane and hit his car. Both cars parked on the side of the road. No one was hurt. Brad was very angry. What should Brad do first?

   A. Shout at the other driver.
   B. Stay calm and check damage to his car.
   C. Call the police.

3. Rita was waiting at a traffic light when the car behind her bumped into her car. She wasn't sure if it was serious. She signaled to the other driver and they pulled over to the side of the road. What should Rita do next?

   A. Call the police.
   B. Exchange contact information with the other driver.
   C. Call her insurance company.

4. Eddie was driving home after work. He didn't stop at the stop sign when he turned onto his street. Another car was driving toward him. He hit the side of the other car. What should Eddie do first?

   A. Pull over to the side of the road.
   B. Get out and talk to the other driver.
   C. Drive away quickly.

4 CHECK ☑ *True* or *False*.

	True	False
1. You don't have to discuss the car accident with the other driver.	☐	☐
2. You have to get the driver's name and address.	☐	☐
3. You don't have to call the police.	☐	☐
4. You have to call your insurance company first.	☐	☐
5. You must say "I'm sorry" about the accident.	☐	☐
6. You must try to stay calm and quiet. You mustn't get angry.	☐	☐

5 REAL-LIFE LESSON. Find out information about car insurance. Ask a family member or go on the Internet. What are the different types of insurance? What kinds of accidents are covered?

_____

_____

_____

_____

_____

_____

_____

_____

_____

_____

Community Connection: The Three Branches of Government

1 **READ** the questions. Choose the best answer. Check your answers on the Internet or with your teacher.

1. Who can vote in the United States?
   - **A.** U.S. citizens
   - **B.** U.S. residents
   - **C.** non-U.S. citizens
   - **D.** U.S. citizens born in the U.S.

2. Who can become a senator or a representative?
   - **A.** U.S. citizens
   - **B.** U.S. residents
   - **C.** non-U.S. citizens
   - **D.** U.S. citizens born in the U.S.

3. Who can become president?
   - **A.** U.S. citizens
   - **B.** U.S. residents
   - **C.** non-U.S. citizens
   - **D.** U.S. citizens born in the U.S.

2 **READ** the article.

★ ★ ★ ★ THE THREE BRANCHES OF GOVERNMENT. ★ ★ ★ ★

The U.S. government has three **branches:** the legislative branch, the judicial branch, and the executive branch.

The legislative branch is the Congress. Congress has two parts: the House of Representatives and the Senate. Citizens of the United States vote for representatives and senators. They meet in the Capitol in Washington, D.C. There are 100 senators. Each senator is **elected** for six years. There are 435 representatives. Each representative is elected for two years. Congress makes the laws for the country and decides how much tax we have to pay. It decides who can immigrate to the United States.

The executive branch is made up of the president, the vice president, and the cabinet. The president is the leader of the country. He is elected for four years. He signs the laws. He also prepares budgets and is head of the military. The cabinet is a small group of people at the top of the government. They give advice to the president. For example, the secretary of defense has responsibility for the military.

The judicial branch is made up of the Supreme Court and the **federal** courts. The courts have to decide the correct meaning of the law and explain it to the people. The Supreme Court is the **highest** court in the United States. It has nine **judges.**

3 CIRCLE the correct answer.

1. What is the executive branch of government?
   A. the Senate
   B. the Congress
   C. the president

2. What is Congress?
   A. the president and the Senate
   B. the president and the cabinet
   C. the Senate and the House of Representatives

3. What does the judicial branch do?
   A. It makes the laws.
   B. It signs the laws.
   C. It explains the laws.

4 FIND these words in the article. Use context to guess their meanings.

1. branches
   A. parts
   B. examples
   C. laws

2. elected
   A. completed
   B. chosen
   C. employed

3. federal
   A. national
   B. international
   C. state

4. highest
   A. most expensive
   B. most intelligent
   C. most important

5. judges
   A. people who make laws
   B. people who decide the meaning of laws
   C. people who change laws

5 REAL-LIFE LESSON. Answer the questions. Check your answers on the Internet or with your teacher.

1. Who is the president of the United States? _____

2. Who is the vice president? _____

3. Who are the senators from your state? _____

4. How many representatives does your state have? _____

Career Connection: Using a Time Sheet

1 **READ.** Jack Wilson works at an office supply store. Read and complete his time sheet.

Employee Time Sheet							
Employee Name	Jack Wilson						
Department	Deliveries						
Start Date	5/19/08						
Day	**Date**	**Start Work**	**Time Out (lunch)**	**Time In (lunch)**	**End Work**	**Total Daily Hours**	**Total Weekly Hours**
Monday	5/19/08	7:30 A.M.	12:00 P.M.	1:00 P.M.	5:00 P.M.	8.5	8.5
Tuesday	5/20/08	8:00 A.M.	12:30 P.M.	1:30 P.M.	5:00 P.M.	8	16.5
Wednesday	5/21/08	7:30 A.M.	12:00 P.M.	1:00 P.M.	5:00 P.M.		
Thursday	5/2208	7:30 A.M.	12:30 P.M.	1:30 P.M.	5:00 P.M.		
Friday	5/23/08	7:30 A.M.	12:00 P.M.	1:00 P.M.	5:00 P.M.		
Saturday	5/24/08	—	—	—	—		
Sunday	5/25/08	—	—	—	—		
Weekly Total							
Total hours							
Pay per hour	$8.00						
Total pay							

2 **TALK** with a partner. Discuss your job (or a job that you know about). Describe your work schedule. Do you have to start early / finish late / work on weekends? Is it important to start work on time at your job?

3 **EDIT.** There are six mistakes. Correct them.

My Work Day

I work as a manager in a fast food restaurant. It is important to be punctual every day. I ~~has~~ *have* to start work at 6:30 A.M. When the employees arrive, they has to put their time cards into a time clock. We doesn't have to wear uniforms at work, but men couldn't have beards or long hair and women with long hair has to wear hair nets. I finish work at 4 P.M. I give the keys to the night manager. She have to stay at work from 4 A.M. until 1 A.M.

 4 **WRITE** a description of your day. Describe the rules in your workplace or school.

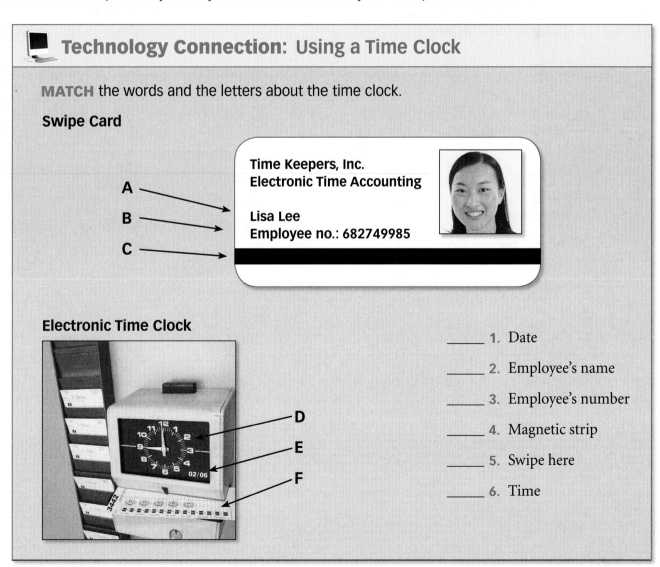

💻 **Technology Connection:** Using a Time Clock

MATCH the words and the letters about the time clock.

Swipe Card

Time Keepers, Inc.
Electronic Time Accounting

Lisa Lee
Employee no.: 682749985

A
B
C

Electronic Time Clock

D
E
F

02/06
3442

_____ 1. Date

_____ 2. Employee's name

_____ 3. Employee's number

_____ 4. Magnetic strip

_____ 5. Swipe here

_____ 6. Time

Practice Test

LISTENING: Listen to the beginning of a conversation. Then listen for the next best sentence. Choose the correct answer.

1. Ⓐ   Ⓑ   Ⓒ
2. Ⓐ   Ⓑ   Ⓒ

LISTENING: Listen to the conversation. Then choose the correct answer.

3. Who are the speakers?
   A. a resident and a manager
   B. a resident and a visitor
   C. two residents

4. What does Jan have to do with her boxes?
   A. leave them in the common area
   B. put them outside
   C. bring them indoors

5. Where can Jan's sister park her car?
   A. in the assigned parking
   B. in front of the building
   C. out back

GRAMMAR: Choose the correct word or phrase to complete each sentence.

6. The handbook says that employees ____ listen to music while they are working.
   A. may not
   B. cannot
   C. must
   D. have to

7. What is the dress code? ____ we wear sneakers to work?
   A. Have
   B. Must not
   C. Can
   D. May not

8. Residents ____ smoke in common areas.
   A. don't have to
   B. have to
   C. must not
   D. must

9. Visitors ____ leave the park by 9 P.M.
   A. must
   B. cannot
   C. don't have to
   D. must not

10. The park is free. Visitors ____ pay.
   A. don't have to
   B. must not
   C. have to
   D. must

VOCABULARY: Choose the best word or phrase to complete the sentence.

11. I don't want to work at night. Can you ____ shifts with me, please?
    A. change
    B. exchange
    C. use
    D. make

12. You must pay a ____ to camp in the park.
    A. cost
    B. ticket
    C. license
    D. fee

13. My cat does not go outside. It stays ____.
    A. out back
    B. indoors
    C. upstairs
    D. outside

14. There are lots of people going up the stairs. The ____ is noisy.
    A. parking
    B. Dumpster
    C. stairwell
    D. laundry room

15. Chang is calling his wife. He's making a ____ call.
    A personal
    B. text
    C. free
    D. work

READING: Read. Choose the correct answer.

All male employees must wear white shirts and ties. In summer, they may wear short-sleeved shirts without a tie. They may not wear T-shirts. Women must wear white blouses or shirts and dark pants. They may not wear jeans or shorts. Employees must wear closed-toe shoes. Sandals are permitted in summer only. Boots are not permitted. Flip-flops and sneakers are prohibited. Female employees may not wear long earrings.

16. Male employees have to wear ____.
    A. sandals
    B. T-shirts
    C. white shirts
    D. short-sleeved shirts

17. Employees may not wear ____.
    A. white blouses
    B. dark pants
    C. sneakers
    D. boots

18. Employees may wear ____.
    A. T-shirts
    B. short-sleeved shirts
    C. boots
    D. long earrings

19. Employees may wear ____ in summer.
    A. jeans
    B. shorts
    C. sandals
    D. flip-flops

20. Do male employees have to wear ties?
    A. Yes, they do.
    B. No, they don't.
    C. Not in summer.
    D. Only in summer.

Lesson 1

1 **MATCH** the words with the pictures. Write the words.

| chest pains | itchy eyes | out of breath | ~~runny nose~~ | skin rash | swollen ankle |

1. *runny nose*
2. _____
3. _____
4. _____
5. _____
6. _____

2 (CIRCLE) the correct answer.

1. Sue has a runny nose. She may have   **a.** allergies   **b.** asthma.

2. Al has a bad rash on his face. He could have   **a.** bronchitis   **b.** eczema.

3. Luz has a bad cough and chest pains. She may have   **a.** bronchitis   **b.** conjunctivitis.

4. Gina's eyes are red and they feel itchy. She must have   **a.** eczema   **b.** conjunctivitis.

5. Bill gets out of breath when he climbs the stairs. He might have   **a.** asthma   **b.** bronchitis.

6. Pam cut her finger and it's swollen. She may need to go to the doctor to get some   **a.** lotion   **b.** antibiotics.

3 **WRITE** sentences.

1. (may, a cold, have) I have a runny nose. ___*I may have a cold.*___

2. (might, asthma, have) Bob is out of breath. _____

3. (might, antibiotics, need) Your foot is swollen. _____

4. (must, itchy, feel) Nick has a rash on his hand. _____

5. (must, conjunctivitis, have) Isabella's eyes are red. _____

6. (could, bronchitis, have) I have a cough. _____

Lesson 2

1 MATCH. What kind of doctor do these people need to see? Write the letters.

1. Linda needs an x-ray of her wrist. She is going to see the ___d___.
2. They need to check his heart. He's going to the _____.
3. My little daughter is sick. We're going to the _____.
4. Yolanda is going to have a baby. She needs to see the _____.
5. Ling has a skin problem. She's going to the _____.
6. Noah needs to do exercises for his back. He's going to see the _____.

a. pediatrician
b. dermatologist
c. physical therapist
d. ~~radiologist~~
e. gynecologist
f. cardiologist

2 WRITE. Use the words in the box to complete the paragraph.

antibiotics	chest	~~cough~~	dermatologist	fever	flu	lotion	pediatrician	rash	runny

My son often gets a (1) ___cough___ and a (2) _____ nose in winter. This

winter he had serious (3) _____ pains and he had a (4) _____,

too—it was over 100° F. I was very worried. So I called my mother and she said he should see the

(5) _____ right away. The doctor said my son might need to take some

(6) _____. Then she noticed a (7) _____ on his hands and she gave me

some (8) _____ for it. She said we might need to see a (9) _____ if

the rash doesn't get better. Then she asked if my son had a stomachache because he might not have

the (10) _____ — it could be an allergy!

3 USE YOUR DICTIONARY. Complete the chart. Then <u>underline</u> the stressed syllable in each word in columns 1 and 2.

Medical field	Doctor	What part of the body?
cardi<u>o</u>logy	cardi<u>o</u>logist	heart
neurology		
gastroenterology		
otolaryngology		
osteopathy		

Lesson 3

1 **LISTEN** to the conversation. Then listen to the question. Fill in the circle for the correct answer.

1. Ⓐ   Ⓑ   Ⓒ
2. Ⓐ   Ⓑ   Ⓒ
3. Ⓐ   Ⓑ   Ⓒ

2 **LISTEN** to the conversation between a doctor and a patient. Complete the chart.

WCD, 21

Symptoms	Illness	Medicine	Instructions

3 **WRITE** the lines of the conversation in the correct order.

Yes, of course. Who is your doctor?

We have Thursday morning at 11:30 A.M. Is that better for you?

Good morning. I'd like to make an appointment, please.

Could you make it a little later, please? Around 10 A.M. would be good.

My doctor is Dr. Roberts. It's for my annual checkup.

I see. Can you come in on Thursday morning at 8:00 A.M.?

Yes, that's fine. Thank you.

Patient: _____

Receptionist: _____

Patient: _____

Receptionist: _____

Patient: _____

Receptionist: _____

Patient: _____

4 **PRACTICE** with a partner. Make up your own conversation about making a doctor's appointment.

Culture and Communication: Starting a Conversation

1 **READ** these ways to start a conversation. Practice them with a partner.

Greetings	Replies
How are you?	Great!
How're you doing?	Good, thanks!
How's it going?	Not bad.
How're you feeling?	Not so good today.

Culture Tip

You can start a conversation with *How are you?* or *How are you doing?* This is not usually a question about someone's health. When someone asks you these questions, it is best to give a brief answer such as *Good or Not bad,* and then follow with another question such as *How about you?*, *What's up?*, or *What's new?*

2 **MATCH** the greetings with the replies. Write the letters

1. It's warm today, isn't it? _____

2. What a nice jacket! _____

3. Are you going to class now? _____

4. Did you watch the game last night? _____

5. What's up? _____

a. Thanks! I bought it yesterday.

b. Nothing special.

c. Yes, I did. It was great!

d. Yes, I'm already late.

e. Yes, and I think it's going to get warmer.

3 **WRITE.** Think of ways to start a conversation in each of these situations. Write an appropriate greeting and reply.

1. You're standing at a bus stop and it's raining. You don't have an umbrella. The bus is already 10 minutes late. Some other people are waiting too.

2. It's Friday afternoon. You're going into the library and you see a classmate. Your classmate is carrying some books.

3. It's Monday morning. You're buying a cup of coffee in the cafeteria. You see your classmate standing in line in front of you.

Lesson 4

1 **COMPLETE** the sentences about Al's past and present habits.

Before	Now
1. I drove to work.	I ride a bicycle.
2. I sat at my desk all day.	I exercise on my lunch break.
3. I ate junk food.	I eat healthy snacks.
4. I didn't drink water every day.	I drink four glasses of water a day.
5. I didn't buy fresh food.	I buy fresh vegetables every week.
6. I didn't check my weight.	I weigh myself once a week.

1. Al __used to drive__ to work, but now he _____rides_____ a bicycle.

2. He _____ at his desk all day, but now he _____ on his lunch break.

3. He _____ junk food, but now he _____ healthy snacks.

4. He _____ water every day, but now he _____ four glasses a day.

5. He _____ fresh food, but now he _____ fresh vegetables every week.

6. He _____ his weight, but now he _____ himself once a week.

2 **COMPLETE** the phrases. Use the words in the box.

frozen	labels	low-calorie	sugar

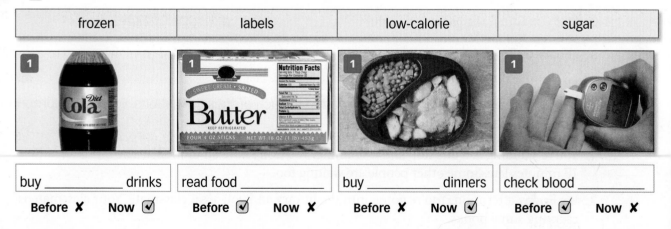

buy _____ drinks	read food _____	buy _____ dinners	check blood _____
Before ✗ **Now** ☑	**Before** ☑ **Now** ✗	**Before** ✗ **Now** ☑	**Before** ☑ **Now** ✗

3 **COMPLETE** the sentences. Use the information in Activity 2 and *used to* or *didn't use to*.

1. I _____*didn't use to*_____ buy _____ drinks.

2. You _____ eat _____ dinners.

3. We _____ read food _____.

4. Ariana _____ check her blood _____.

Lesson 5

1 MATH. Read the nutrition label for Crispy Crackers. Answer the questions.

Nutrition Facts
Serving Size 2 crackers
Servings per container 20

Amount Per Serving

Calories 70	Calories from Fat 10

% Daily Value*

Total Fat 1g	1%
Saturated Fat 0g	0%
Trans Fat 0g	0%
Cholesterol 0mg	0%
Sodium 110mg	4%
Total Carbohydrate 8g	3%
Dietary Fiber 2g	8%
Sugars .3g	0%
Protein 1g	2%

*Percent Daily Values are based on a 2,000 calorie diet. Your daily values may be higher or lower depending on your calorie needs.

	Crispy Crackers	Your Favorite Food
1. How many servings are in this package?	_____	_____
2. How many calories are in one serving?	_____	_____
3. How many calories are in the whole package?	_____	_____
4. How much salt is in one serving?	_____	_____
5. How much salt is in the whole package?	_____	_____
6. Is this product high or low in fat?	_____	_____

2 REAL-LIFE LESSON. Read a nutrition label for a favorite food you eat often. Complete the chart. How does your favorite food compare to the nutrition label in Activity 1?

3 COMPLETE the paragraph with information about yourself.

When I was younger, I used to eat _____, but now I don't. I usually eat _____ every day/ week. I didn't use to _____ in my free time, but now I do. I _____ every day / week / weekend. I used to play _____. But now I don't. I play _____ or _____ instead. I used to be _____ when I was a child, but now I'm not. I think I'm _____ now.

4 READ the clues. Complete the crossword puzzle.

Across

1. I don't eat candy anymore because I'm on a ___.
3. I want to lose weight, so I eat ___ yogurt.
4. I used to eat meat, but now I'm a ___.
5. I don't eat salt because I have high blood ___.

Down

1. I need to eat sugar-free jam because I have ___.
2. I can't eat peanut butter because I'm ___ to nuts.

Family Connection: Completing a Medical History Form

1 **LABEL** the pictures with the names of the organs.

heart—pumps blood around your body	
larynx—part of your throat	
liver—cleans your blood	
lungs—you breathe through them	
pancreas—produces insulin, helps to digest food	
stomach—digests food	

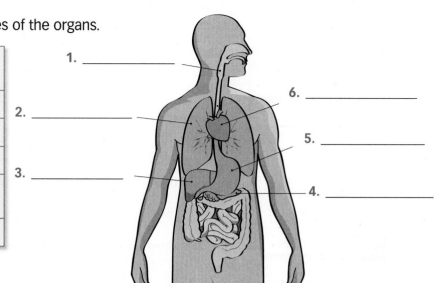

1. _____
2. _____
3. _____
4. _____
5. _____
6. _____

2 **COMPLETE** the chart. Which organ goes with each illness or medical condition?

Illness/condition	Symptoms	Organ
1. hepatitis	skin can turn yellow	*liver*
2. asthma	difficulty breathing	
3. diabetes	not enough insulin	
4. heartburn	pain after eating	
5. laryngitis	difficulty speaking	
6. angina	chest pains	

3 **COMPLETE** the medical history form. Use the information given.

James Carlos Gutierrez and his wife, Marta Gutierrez, live at 124 South Main Street, Fairfield, Connecticut 06824. Their phone number is 203-555-6182. Their e-mail address is jcg@online.org. They have one daughter. Her name is Gina. She was born on April 16, 2002. She has received vaccinations against measles, mumps, and rubella. She has asthma and is allergic to aspirin. She is not currently taking any medications.

Child Medical History Form

Name of child _____
                                  last   first   middle

Date of Birth (MM/DD/YY) _____

Names of parents:

Mother _____
                                  last   first   middle

Father _____
                                  last   first   middle

Address _____
                              street   city   state   zip

Phone number (_____) _____   E-mail _____

Emergency contact number (_____) _____

1. Allergies to medications _____

    Other allergies _____

2. Vaccinations and immunizations _____

3. Serious injuries or operations _____

4. Current medical conditions (diabetes, asthma)

    _____

5. Is your child taking any medications? Please list.

    _____

Date _____

---

4 **DISCUSS** with a partner.

1. Why is it useful to fill out a medical history form for your child?

2. In what situations could it be useful?

3. Where should you keep a copy of this form?

5 **REAL-LIFE LESSON.** Interview a friend or family member about their visit to a doctor. What kinds of questions did the doctor ask? What kind of information did the doctor need? What kinds of questions can you ask your doctor when you are sick? Make a list.

Community Connection: Understanding a Prescription

1 **READ** the information about the community health center.

http://www.communitychs.org/

COMMUNITY HEALTH CENTER SERVICES

Hours of operation: Monday–Thursday 8:30 A.M.–7:00 P.M. • Friday 8:30 A.M.–5:00 P.M. • Saturday 9:00 A.M.–12:00 Noon

At Community Health Center, we deliver quality health care to thousands of community residents. Whether you're a long-time resident or you're new to the area, we're your health center. Our doctors and nurses offer many services, including pediatrics, adult medicine, eye exams, dental care, and nutrition.

We can answer your questions about insurance coverage, choosing a doctor, or making an appointment. When you receive a prescription from one of our providers, you can get immediate and professional service from our pharmacists. We will help you understand how to take your medication and talk to your health provider if necessary.

Community Health Center

2 **WRITE** ✓ (yes) or ✗ (no) for what you can and can't do at this community health center.

1. _____ You can get advice about diet.

2. _____ You can see a dentist.

3. _____ You can get insurance.

4. _____ You can make an appointment to see a doctor.

5. _____ You can get medication.

6. _____ You can ask questions about your medication.

3 **READ** the list of illnesses. Which could you treat with over-the-counter medicine? Which might need prescription medicine from a doctor? Check ☑ the answers.

	Over-the-counter	Prescription
1. asthma	☐	☐
2. cough	☐	☐
3. diabetes	☐	☐
4. headache	☐	☐
5. heartburn	☐	☐
6. backache	☐	☐
7. sore throat	☐	☐

4 **READ** the label. Circle the correct answer.

1. Take one tablet every 8 hours.
    a. Take three tablets every 24 hours.
    b. Take two tablets every 24 hours.

2. Take this medication with plenty of water.
    a. You must drink water with this drug.
    b. You can drink water with this drug.

3. Avoid alcohol when taking this drug.
    a. Do not drink alcohol.
    b. It's okay to drink alcohol.

4. This drug may impair your ability to drive.
    a. You should not drive a car.
    b. It's okay to drive a car.

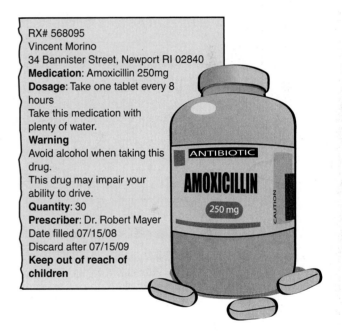

RX# 568095
Vincent Morino
34 Bannister Street, Newport RI 02840
Medication: Amoxicillin 250mg
Dosage: Take one tablet every 8 hours
Take this medication with plenty of water.
Warning
Avoid alcohol when taking this drug.
This drug may impair your ability to drive.
Quantity: 30
Prescriber: Dr. Robert Mayer
Date filled 07/15/08
Discard after 07/15/09
Keep out of reach of children

5 **REAL-LIFE LESSON.** Go to a drugstore. Find the names of three different over-the-counter medicines. What are they for? What is the dosage? What are the directions? What are the warnings?

_____

_____

_____

_____

_____

_____

Career Connection: Calling in Sick

1 **READ** the company rules for sick leave. Are they the same as rules in your place of work?

> **Company Rules for Sick Leave**
>
> - Employees are allowed 5 days a year as paid leave for sickness.
>
> - Employees must telephone the manager on the first day of absence, before 10:00 A.M.
>
> - Sick leave of up to two days is permitted without a doctor's note. Longer periods require a note from a doctor.
>
> - When you return to work, your manager will interview you and fill out a sickness absence form.

2 **READ** the rules in Activity 1 again. Circle *True* or *False*.

1. You can be sick for five days a year without losing any pay.	True	False
2. You don't have to call the manager if you're only sick for one day.	True	False
3. You can be out sick for two days without a note from a doctor.	True	False
4. You need a note from a doctor if you are sick for a week.	True	False
5. You need to talk to your manager about your absence.	True	False

3 **READ** the conversation. Complete the phone message memo.

Ron:	Hi. Could I leave a message for the manager, please?
Desk clerk:	Yes, of course. What's your name?
Ron:	My name is Ron Harris. I'm the assistant reservations clerk.
Desk clerk:	And what is your message?
Ron:	I'm calling in sick today because I have a bad headache. I might have a cold. But I'm sure I can come to work tomorrow.
Desk clerk:	Okay. I'll give him the message.
Ron:	Thanks very much.
Desk clerk:	No problem. . .I hope you feel better soon!

PHONE MESSAGE
- - - - - - - - - - - - - - - - - - - -

For: _____

From: _____

Message: _____

_____

_____

_____

_____

4 **PRACTICE** a conversation with a partner. Student A calls in sick. Student B is the manager. Use information about yourself. Write the conversation in your notebook. Then exchange roles.

5 EDIT. The paragraph has six mistakes. Find the mistakes and correct them.

Sam ~~did~~ used to work as a cab driver. He use to drive hotel guests to the airport. He

enjoyed the work, but he used eat a lot of fast food and didn't used to exercise much. His doctor

said he might to get heart disease. Now he works as an assistant night manager in the hotel.

He walks around the hotel and often takes the stairs. He thinks he is might be healthier now.

💻 Technology Connection: Finding Health Advice Online

MyPyramid.gov (www.mypyramid.gov) is a website created by the U.S. Department of Agriculture to provide information about health and diet.

A Go to the website. Click on "Inside the Pyramid" in the list on the left side of the website. Then click on the parts of the pyramid to find out what the different-colored parts of the pyramid mean. Write the answers below.

1. _____
2. _____
3. _____

6. _____
5. _____
4. _____

B Next, click on "MyPyramid Plan." Enter your age, weight, and height to find the amount of each food group you need daily. Write the answers below.

_____

_____

> **Be Careful!** Be careful when you research health advice online. Check that the website is from a reliable source.

Practice Test

LISTENING: Listen to the conversation. Then listen to the question. Choose the correct answer.

1. (A)   (B)   (C)   2. (A)   (B)   (C)

LISTENING: Listen to the conversation. Then choose the correct answer.

3. What symptom does the patient have?
   - A. cough
   - B. fever
   - C. runny nose

4. What illness might the patient have?
   - A. asthma
   - B. bronchitis
   - C. eczema

5. What medication might the patient need?
   - A. eye drops
   - B. antacid tablets
   - C. an antibiotic

GRAMMAR: Choose the correct word or phrase to complete each sentence.

6. Freddy has a runny nose. He ____ the flu.
   - A. might have
   - B. might to
   - C. might be
   - D. might has

7. You have red eyes. Your eyes ____ itchy.
   - A. must have
   - B. must feel
   - C. must do
   - D. must to

8. I ____ eat frozen dinners.
   - A. use to
   - B. used
   - C. used to
   - D. use

9. Al didn't ____ exercise every day.
   - A. used
   - B. used to
   - C. use to
   - D. use

10. Al and Kate used to eat ice cream every day, but now they ____.
    - A. don't
    - B. didn't
    - C. don't use to
    - D. didn't use to

VOCABULARY: Choose the best word or phrase to complete the sentence.

11. Francine has a bad rash on her arm. She thinks it might be ____.
    - A. bronchitis
    - B. asthma
    - C. conjunctivitis
    - D. eczema

12. I think my ear might be infected. Do you think I need ____?
    - A. a lotion
    - B. eye drops
    - C. antacid tablets
    - D. antibiotics

13. Sam has problems with his heart. He needs to see a _____.
   A. physical therapist
   B. gynecologist
   C. dermatologist
   D. cardiologist

14. These vegetables aren't fresh. They're _____.
   A. vegetarian
   B. low fat
   C. frozen
   D. high calorie

15. You should read the _____ on every package of food.
   A. diet
   B. label
   C. nutrition
   D. calories

READING: Read. Choose the correct answer.

Are Sugar-Free Foods Good for You?

Many foods in your local supermarket, such as jam, jelly, and soda, are labeled sugar free, but they still taste sweet. Why? Because they use artificial sweeteners that do not add extra calories to your diet. As part of a calorie-controlled diet, they might help you to lose weight. They might also cause less damage to your teeth. However, they are not always healthier. One problem is that they contain artificial ingredients that may be harmful if you eat them in large quantities or over a long period of time. Another problem is that people may eat more of these foods because they think they are healthier than other foods. In fact, it's healthier to reduce your intake of sweet foods and eat a balanced diet.

16. What is the main topic of this article?
   A. how to lose weight
   B. how to reduce sugar in your diet
   C. the advantages of eating sugar-free foods
   D. whether or not sugar-free foods are healthy

17. What is one argument for sugar-free foods?
   A. They contain sugar.
   B. They have fewer calories.
   C. They taste better.
   D. They don't taste sweet.

18. What is one argument against sugar-free foods?
   A. They might help you lose weight.
   B. They damage your teeth.
   C. They don't taste sweet.
   D. They may not always be healthy.

19. The article says that artificial sweeteners _____.
   A. do not taste as sweet as sugar
   B. do not have as many calories as sugar
   C. do not help you lose weight
   D. are healthier than sugar

20. The article says that it is healthier to _____.
   A. eat less sugar-free food
   B. eat less sweet food
   C. eat less food
   D. eat more food

Lesson 1

1 **READ** the sentences. Cross out the words in italics. Write words with the same meaning from the box.

donate	get in shape	help out	~~join~~	sign up	tutor

join
1. I'm going to ~~become a member~~ of the PTA.

2. Luisa is going to *register* for art classes this spring.

3. Alex is going to *give individual lessons to* teenagers after school.

4. Sam is going to *give* blood at the health center on Friday.

5. Jody is going to *exercise regularly* at the gym.

6. Frank is going to *do some work* at the community center.

2 **COMPLETE** the sentences. Use the verbs in parentheses and infinitives of the verbs from the box in Activity 1.

1. I have some old books and toys. I ____plan to donate____ (plan) them to the community center.

2. Dan's neighbors need some help. He _____ (intend) the neighborhood volunteer group.

3. Boris needs computer skills for his job. He _____ (need) for computer classes this fall.

4. Katrina has some extra time this weekend. She _____ (would like) at the homeless shelter.

5. Julie is good at math. She _____ (want) kids after school.

6. Brad doesn't exercise very much. This year he _____ (plan) at the local gym.

Lesson 2

1 **CIRCLE** the correct verb.

1. Ivana teaches after school every day. She *likes* / *would like* to tutor teenagers.

2. Henry volunteers every week. He *likes* / *would like* to help other people.

3. Jose and Amelia haven't started school yet. They *like* / *would like* to study math.

4. Bernie doesn't like to study alone. She *likes* / *would like* to join a study group.

5. Yang cooks meals at the homeless shelter. He *likes* / *would like* to help out in his free time.

6. Lam and Gina don't usually buy vegetables at the supermarket. They *like* / *would like* to go to the Farmer's Market.

2 **COMPLETE** the paragraph. Use the words in the box.

animal shelter	~~farmer's market~~	homeless shelter	nature center
clinic	fitness center	library	youth center

Our family is always very busy in our free time. On Saturday morning, we all go shopping at the (1) ___farmer's market___. Then we usually visit the (2) _____ to return books and check out new ones. On Sunday, we sometimes take a walk on a trail at the (3) _____. I go to the (4) _____ twice a week to run on the exercise machines, and my children go to the (5) _____ to play soccer and volleyball. Today, there's a blood drive at the local health (6) _____, and we're going to donate blood.

My children love to take care of animals, and they often help out at the (7) _____ _____ during school vacation. We also like to do some volunteer activities together as a family. On Thanksgiving and at Christmas, we help to cook meals at the (8) _____ _____.

Lesson 3

1 LISTEN to the beginning of a conversation. Then listen for the next best sentence. Fill in the circle for the correct answer.

1. Ⓐ Ⓑ Ⓒ
2. Ⓐ Ⓑ Ⓒ
3. Ⓐ Ⓑ Ⓒ

2 LISTEN to the conversation between Kathy and Sam. Circle *True* or *False*.

1. Thanksgiving is Sam's favorite holiday.	True	False
2. Sam usually eats turkey on Thanksgiving.	True	False
3. Sam usually spends Thanksgiving with his family.	True	False
4. Kathy invites Sam to spend Thanksgiving with her family.	True	False
5. Sam turns down the invitation.	True	False

3 NUMBER the lines of the conversation in the correct order.

___1___ Paula: Hi, Diane. What are you doing for Thanksgiving?

_____ Paula: Great.

_____ Paula: I'd really like to, but I promised to volunteer at the homeless shelter.

_____ Diane: That sounds really great. I'd like to do that next year.

_____ Diane: I plan to have dinner with my family. Do you want to join us?

4 PRACTICE. Make up your own conversation asking about plans for a holiday. Practice with a partner.

5 MATH. Read Sally's entertainment budget for September and October. Calculate her total expenses for each month.

September	October
Swimming $10	Dinner with friends $32
DVD rental $5	Movie $8
Lunch with friends $15	Concert $30
Total _____	Total _____

Sally's budget is $65 per month. How much was she over or under her budget each month?

September _____   October _____

Culture and Communication: Making, Accepting, and Declining Invitations

1 **READ** about ways to make, accept, and decline invitations.

Ways to make an invitation
Do you want to go to the movies tonight?
We're having a party on Saturday. Can you come?
How about joining us for dinner tomorrow night?
Would you like to join us for lunch tomorrow? (*formal*)

Ways to accept an invitation
Sure!
I'd/We'd love to.
Sounds great?
Thank you!

Ways to decline an invitation
I'd/We'd love to, but…
I'd/We'd like to, but…
Thank you for asking, but…
Thank you, but I'm not able to attend. (*formal*)

Culture Tip
People in the United States sometimes make general invitations as a sign of friendship. They might say, *Let's get together soon.* In these cases, the answer can also be general, for example, *Sure! Let's do that.* If there is a specific invitation, you should accept or decline. You don't have to go into detail about your reasons for declining. A general reason is good enough. For example, *I'd love to, but I'm busy on that day.*

2 **READ.** Julie was out last night. When she got home, she had three voice mail messages.

1. Hi, Julie. This is Angela. Do you want to come to a party tomorrow night? It starts at 6:30 and it's at Pete's house. Give me a call. It's 201-555-4321.

2. Hi, Julie. This is Pete. I'm having a party on Saturday. Can you come? 6:30 at my house. My number is 212-555-6548.

3. Hi, Julie. This is Sam. Do you want to go to the movies with me tomorrow night? The movie starts at 7. I'll pick you up at 6:30. Okay? My number is 201-555-3576.

3 Julie called back each of her friends, but they were all out. Write the messages she left.

Tip
When you leave a voice message, remember to say who the message is for, your name, and a number to call you back.

1. _____

_____

2. _____

_____

3. _____

_____

Lesson 4

1 **COMPLETE** the chart. What form follows each verb? Write the verbs in the box in the correct column.

~~dislike~~	enjoy	finish	hate	intend	like	love	plan	want

Infinitive	Infinitive or gerund	Gerund
		dislike

2 **WRITE** the gerund or the infinitive of the verb in parentheses.

1. I intend _____*to hang out*_____ (hang out) at the beach all summer.

2. I dislike _____ (waste) money on popcorn.

3. Marcia enjoys _____ (go) to music festivals.

4. We're planning _____ (hike) in the mountains this weekend.

5. I'm going to finish _____ (read) my book tonight.

6. Sandy would like _____ (make) new friends at the party.

3 **COMPLETE** the sentences with information about you. Use gerunds or infinitives.

1. I love _____, but I hate_____.

2. I dislike _____ and I can't stand _____.

3. I want to _____, but I don't intend to _____.

4. I enjoy _____, but I prefer _____.

Lesson 5

1 WRITE questions. Then write answers with information about yourself.

Example: *Do you like window shopping? Yes, I do.*

Questions   **Answers**

1. hate/get up early

_____ ?   _____

2. dislike/waste money

_____ ?   _____

3. like/eat out in restaurants

_____ ?   _____

 2 USE YOUR DICTIONARY. Check the pronunciation of the words. Which word has the same vowel sound as the first word? Circle one word in each group.

1. like   **a.** make   **b.** find   **c.** think

2. walk   **a.** work   **b.** hang   **c.** fall

3. waste   **a.** hate   **b.** like   **c.** stand

4. spend   **a.** hate   **b.** help   **c.** hear

WCD, 26

3 PRONUNCIATION. Listen and circle the stressed word in each answer.

1. A: Do you like watching soccer?   B: No, but I love watching baseball.

2. A: Do you like watching soccer?   B: No, but I love playing soccer.

3. A: Do you like watching soccer?   B: Yes, I love watching soccer.

4 COMPLETE the story. Write the words in the puzzle. Then find the mystery word in the puzzle.

I like to (5) _____*spend*_____ money, but I don't like to (6) _____ time. I (2) _____ meeting people, but I (1) _____ going to parties. I like to (4) _____ to music, but I don't like to (3) _____ on the phone. On weekends, I like to (7) _____ home with my cat.

Family Connection: Taking a Family Road Trip

1 **READ** the words for different parts of a car.

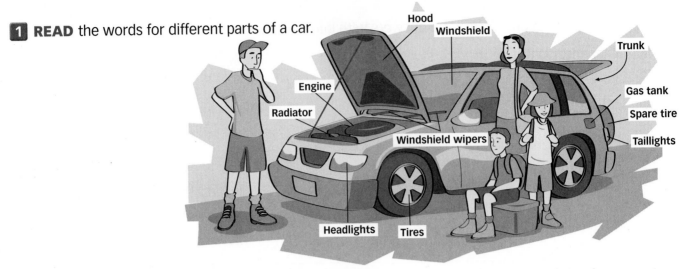

2 **COMPLETE** the sentences. Use the words in Activity 1.

The Rodriguez family is planning to go on a road trip. Andy is going to check the car before their trip. First, Andy plans to open the (1) ___*hood*___ to look at the (2) _____.
He wants to check the oil and the (3) _____ fluid. Then he intends to check the air pressure in the (4) _____. He also needs to check the (5) _____ in the (6) _____. Then he's going to wash the (7) _____ and make sure there is enough fluid for the (8) _____. After that, he needs to make sure the (9) _____ and (10) _____ are working.
Finally, he is going to fill up the (11) _____.

3 **MATCH** the pictures with the sentences.

1. _____ He got a flat tire.   2. _____ His car broke down.   3. _____ He has a dead battery.

4 READ. What did Andy forget to check in his car?

Is Your Car Ready for a Road Trip?

Millions of people take road trips in the United States every year. Before you leave, check your car and make sure everything is working.

It is a good idea to take your car to your local garage and ask a mechanic to check the engine and change the oil. You can also do some important checks yourself. First, open the hood and check the oil level and the radiator fluid. Next, check the windshield wiper fluid and the windshield wipers. Finally, check all the tires and the tire pressure, including the spare tire.

There are a few things that you should have in the car for an emergency. Your emergency kit should include: jumper cables for a dead battery; a gallon of water for radiator problems, or for hot weather; a can of Fix-a-Flat® and a spare tire in case of a flat; a flashlight with extra batteries; and road maps. A cell phone is very helpful, but remember that it may not work in all areas.

Take some time to prepare for your road trip, no matter how far you are going. It will help you to have a safer and more enjoyable trip.

5 CHECK ☑ *True, False,* or *Not mentioned* if the information is not in the text.

	True	False	Not mentioned
1. Many people take road trips every year.	☐	☐	☐
2. Most people forget to check their cars.	☐	☐	☐
3. You need to check the oil level in your car.	☐	☐	☐
4. You don't need to check the tire pressure.	☐	☐	☐
5. You should take your cell phone on a road trip.	☐	☐	☐
6. Many cars break down on a road trip.	☐	☐	☐

6 REAL-LIFE LESSON Plan a road trip for yourself or your family. Look up the information in an atlas or on the Internet. Where are you planning to go? How long will it take to get there? What do you need to take with you? What checks do you need to make on your car?

Community Connection: Volunteering

1 **READ** the information in the bar chart. Circle the answers to the questions.

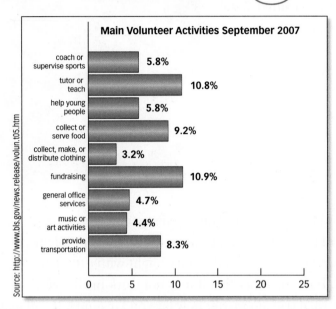

1. What information does the chart show?

   a. reasons for volunteering   **b.** volunteering activities   **c.** skills needed by volunteers

2. Which of these three volunteer activities was the most popular?

   a. sports   **b.** music or art   **c.** fundraising

3. Which of these three volunteer activities was the least popular?

   a. fundraising   **b.** sports   **c.** transportation

4. What percentage were involved in fundraising?

   a. almost 12%   **b.** almost 11%   **c.** almost 10%

2 **TALK** with a partner. Which of the volunteer activities in Activity 1 would you like to do? Which of them would you be good at? Which of them would you enjoy doing? Why? Complete the sentences.

I would like to _____

I am good at _____

I enjoy _____ because _____

_____

3 **REAL-LIFE LESSON.** Find out about volunteer organizations in your community. What kind of volunteer activities do they need?

Name of organization: _____

Kind of activities needed: _____

4 COMPLETE the volunteer application with your information.

Volunteer Application

Thanks for your interest in volunteering with us. Our organization depends on your hard work!

Please print clearly.

Name _____

                               Last   First   Middle

Street _____ City _____ State _____ Zip _____

Work phone _____ Home phone _____

E-mail _____ Date of birth _____ / _____ / _____

How often would you like to volunteer? ☐ daily ☐ weekly ☐ monthly ☐ special events

Please specify times you are available. _____

> Check ☑ up to three volunteer activities you are interested in.
>
> ☐ Fundraising: Call banks, companies, families, and individuals to get donations.
>
> ☐ Graphic designers: Design posters, flyers, advertisements, newsletters.
>
> ☐ Distribution: Hand out flyers, advertisements, and newsletters.
>
> ☐ Facilities: Gardening, building maintenance and repair.

How did you hear about us?

_____

_____

Why do you want to volunteer with us?

_____

_____

Special qualifications (for example, education, languages) interests, and hobbies.

_____

_____

_____

Signature _____ Date _____

Career Connection: Setting Career Goals

1 READ the information about setting career goals.

Setting Career Goals

One way to plan for the future is to set goals. Goals can help you to decide what is most important in your career and how to get the kind of job you can really be good at and enjoy.

Goals may be either short-term or long-term. First, think about your short-term goals. Where do you want to be next year? Short-term goals might include getting a promotion at work or improving your job skills. Short-term goals are often a stop along the way to long-term goals.

Next, think about your long-term goals. Where do you want to be ten years from now? Long-term goals might include earning a higher salary, taking on new responsibilities at work, getting a new job, or starting a business.

Then use your goals to develop a career action plan. The action plan describes the steps you will take to reach your goals.

2 READ the example. Then complete your own career action plan.

Career Action Plan	
Long-term goal: I want to get a job in a senior care center.	
Short-term goals:	**Action:**
1. Take classes in health care for seniors.	Get information from the community college, register for classes.
2. Do research on senior care centers in my city.	Use the Internet or go to the library. Collect addresses and useful contact information.
3. Do some volunteer work at senior care centers.	Find names of volunteer organizations and fill out an application.

Long-term goal:	
Short-term goals:	**Action:**
1.	
2.	
3.	
4.	

3 WRITE a paragraph about your future career goals. Answer these questions.

What do you enjoy doing at work? What do you plan to study in the future? What job or new activity do you hope to do in the future?

4 **EDIT.** The paragraph has six mistakes. Correct them.

Shu-lin hopes ~~being~~ _to be_ a vet. She loves animals and she enjoys to take care of them. She has three dogs at home and she likes take them on a walk every morning. She loves to spending her free time at the animal shelter. She hopes to getting a job as a volunteer there this summer. She intends to take some courses in animal health and nutrition at the community college this fall. In the future, she would likes to become a full-time vet in her local community.

Technology Connection: Using an Online Community Notice Board

COMMUNITY NOTICE BOARD

Home
Community
Housing
Jobs
For Sale

Classes   Activities   Musicians
Events   Childcare   Rideshare
Groups   Lost and Found   Volunteers
Pets

Which heading would you click to get information for the following situations?

1. You want to find a studio to record music. _____

2. You want to get a cat. _____

3. You want to join a reading group. _____

4. You want to volunteer at a homeless shelter. _____

5. You want to find someone to commute to work with. _____

Practice Test

LISTENING: Listen to the beginning of a conversation. Then listen for the next best sentence. Choose the correct answer.

WCD, 27

1. Ⓐ   Ⓑ   Ⓒ

2. Ⓐ   Ⓑ   Ⓒ

LISTENING: Listen to the conversation. Then choose the correct answer.

WCD, 28

3. Which holiday are they speaking about?
   A. Fourth of July
   B. Thanksgiving
   C. New Year's Day

4. What does Hong usually do on this holiday?
   A. He has a party.
   B. He stays home with his family.
   C. He watches fireworks.

5. What does Tina invite Hong to do?
   A. to have dinner
   B. to open cards and gifts
   C. to watch fireworks

GRAMMAR: Choose the correct word or phrase to complete each sentence.

6. Linda intends ____ up for art classes this year.
   A. sign
   B. to sign
   C. signing
   D. signs

7. I ____ to help out at the senior center.
   A. would
   B. would to like
   C. would likes
   D. would like

8. Tony dislikes ____ money on a movie.
   A. to spend
   B. spending
   C. spend
   D. spends

9. Do you enjoy ____ small talk at parties?
   A. make
   B. to make
   C. making
   D. makes

10. A: Can you come to our party tomorrow night?
    B: _____
    A. I'd love to.
    B. I love to.
    C. Yes, I love.
    D. Yes, I do.

VOCABULARY: Choose the best word or phrase to complete each sentence.

11. Frank is going to ____ blood at the medical center.
    A. join
    B. take
    C. donate
    D. volunteer

12. Gary is going to ____ for computer classes.
    A. donate
    B. help out
    C. join
    D. sign up

13. I'm planning to _____ with my friends this weekend.
    A. hang out
    B. attend
    C. help out
    D. enjoy

14. I don't eat out in restaurants. I don't like to _____ money.
    A. spend
    B. save
    C. get
    D. take

15. I don't like parties because I'm not good at _____.
    A. shopping
    B. window shopping
    C. small talk
    D. spending money

READING: Read. Choose the correct answer.

Becoming a Volunteer

When I moved to this neighborhood, the first thing I did was to sign up to be a volunteer. Let me tell you why. Volunteer work is a great way to meet other people. Volunteers work together and set goals. You'll love being part of a team. You can also discover what kinds of things you enjoy doing. Volunteer work is not difficult. Volunteers help each other to learn new skills. A volunteer job gives you ideas about your career goals. Volunteering gives you a sense of responsibility because people really depend on you. You can learn how to help other people. We need more volunteers at the Community Care Center. Join us and become part of our team. You only need to donate a little of your time each week. Help us to build a strong community. You can make a difference.

16. The main topic of this paragraph is _____.
    A. new skills
    B. volunteer work
    C. team work
    D. responsibility

17. Which one is not true? Volunteer work _____.
    A. helps you to meet other people
    B. helps the community
    C. gives you ideas about your career goals
    D. takes a lot of time

18. Which one is an opinion?
    A. The writer signed up to be a volunteer.
    B. Volunteering is a great way to meet other people.
    C. Volunteers learn new skills.
    D. Volunteers work together and set goals.

19. Which one is a fact?
    A. Volunteers work together.
    B. Volunteer work is not difficult.
    C. You'll love being part of a team.
    D. You can make a difference.

20. What is the purpose of the paragraph?
    A. to give information about volunteer work
    B. to describe the writer's volunteer work
    C. to explain why volunteer work is important
    D. to persuade the reader to become a volunteer

Lesson 1

1 **COMPLETE** the phrases. Use the words in the box.

affordable housing	air pollution	~~crime~~
public transportation	trash collection services	traffic

too much ___crime___

not enough _____

not enough _____

too much _____

not enough _____

too much _____

2 **COMPLETE** the sentences. Use *too many, too much,* and *enough*.

1. There isn't ___enough___ housing in our city. We need more apartments.

2. Oak Street is dangerous. There are _____ cars.

3. I don't like Los Angeles. There is _____ traffic.

4. Is there _____ air pollution in your city, or is the air clean?

5. Kim wants to plant some vegetables. Is there _____ space in the yard?

6. Our neighborhood isn't safe. There is _____ crime.

7. We can't buy a new car right now. There isn't _____ money.

8. I don't want to drive on that road. There are _____ accidents.

Lesson 2

1 **MATCH** the letters and the words.

1. __*a*__ bridge

2. _____ crosswalk

3. _____ factory

4. _____ parking garage

5. _____ playground

6. _____ smoke

2 **WRITE.** Look at the picture in Activity 1. Complete the paragraph with *too* or *enough* and the adjectives in parentheses.

This is River City. It has a lot of problems. For example, a lot of people live in River City

and the schools are (1) _____*too crowded*_____ (crowded). The playground is

(2) _____ (small), too. There aren't enough parking spaces because

the parking garage isn't (3) _____ (big). Also, the bridge isn't

(4) _____ (wide). There's a lot of traffic on it because it's

(5) _____ (narrow). There's too much pollution in River City, too.

The factory is (6) _____ (close) to the city. It isn't

(7) _____ (far) from the city, so there's a lot of smoke everywhere.

The river is (8) _____ (dirty). You can't swim in it. The trash cans aren't

(9) _____ (big), so the playground isn't (10) _____ (clean)

for the children.

Lesson 3

WCD, 29

1 **LISTEN.** Match the situations to the pictures. Write the numbers under the pictures.

WCD, 30

2 **LISTEN** to the conversation. Then listen to the question. Fill in the circle for the correct answer.

1. Ⓐ   Ⓑ   Ⓒ

2. Ⓐ   Ⓑ   Ⓒ

3. Ⓐ   Ⓑ   Ⓒ

3 **COMPLETE** the conversation. Use the words in the box.

check it for you	I'm afraid	I see some	too high	You're welcome

A: Is something wrong?

B: Well, _____ there's a problem with the check.

A: Oh. What's the problem?

B: Well, the total is _____. And _____

     extra charges. We didn't order pasta or dessert.

A: Sorry about that. I'll _____.

B: Thank you very much.

A: _____. I'll be right back.

4 **PRACTICE** the conversation with a partner.

Culture and Communication: Making Polite Requests

1 **READ** the sentences. Are they polite or impolite? Check ☑ the correct box.

		Polite	Impolite
1.	Turn off the lights.	☐	☐
2.	Would you please turn off the lights?	☐	☐
3.	Could you speak a little louder?	☐	☐
4.	Stop smoking!	☐	☐
5.	Would you mind not smoking?	☐	☐
6.	You're talking too loud.	☐	☐
7.	Would you please talk more quietly?	☐	☐
8.	Don't turn here! Turn there!	☐	☐
9.	Would you please turn here?	☐	☐

2 **READ** the conversations. Then practice with a partner.

1

Mr. Green: Amy, these glasses aren't clean enough. <u>Would you mind</u> washing them again, please?

Amy: Sure, Mr. Green.

2

Raul: Ms. Burk, the classroom is too noisy. <u>Could you</u> close the door?

Ms. Burk: Of course, Raul.

3

Rob: Sir, there's too much traffic on Oak Street. <u>Would you please</u> take Bay Street?

Driver: No problem, sir.

4

Mark: Hey, Jane, these instructions aren't clear enough. <u>Do you mind</u> writing them again?

Jane: I'd be happy to.

3 **PRACTICE** with a partner. Read the situations. Then have conversations. Use the expressions in the Culture Tip box above. Change the impolite requests to polite requests.

Example: *A:* It's too cold in here. Would you mind closing a window?
                B: Okay.

Situations	**Impolite Requests**
1. The classroom is too cold.	Close the window.
2. Your neighbor's music is too loud.	Turn the music down.
3. The hotel room is too noisy.	Give me another room.
4. You can't hear your teacher.	Speak a little louder.
5. There aren't enough towels in your hotel room.	Give me more towels.
6. The student next to you is tapping a pencil.	Stop doing that.

Lesson 4

1 **MATCH** the pictures and the phrases. Write the letters.

a. recycling	b. ~~insulating the water pipes~~	c. reusing paper
d. unplugging the appliances	e. turning down the thermostat	f. weatherproofing

1. _b_

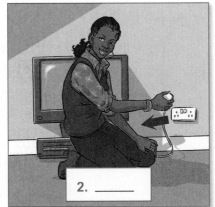

2. _____

3. _____

4. _____

5. _____

6. _____

2 **COMPLETE** the sentences. Use the correct form of the verbs in parentheses.

1. _____Turning_____ (Turn) down the thermostat _____saves_____ (save) money.

2. _____ (Pay) your bills online _____ (be) easy.

3. _____ (Turn) off your computer at night _____ (reduce) your energy bill.

4. _____ (Reuse) paper _____ (help) the environment.

5. _____ (Weatherproof) your doors _____ (keep) your house warmer.

6. _____ (Unplug) your appliances _____ (lower) your electricity bill.

Lesson 5

1 WRITE the negative form of the gerund. Then match the sentence parts.

1. Fix: _Not fixing_ __d__   a. the water while you brush your teeth wastes water.

2. Close: _____ _____   b. the refrigerator door wastes electricity.

3. Turn off: _____ _____   c. a big car is good for the environment.

4. Drive: _____ _____   d. ~~leaky faucets is a bad idea.~~

5. Leave: _____ _____   e. your dishwasher when it's half empty can save energy.

6. Use: _____ _____   f. the lights on when you go out can cut down on your energy use.

2 MATH. Read the formulas. Then calculate the costs.

> How much does it cost to use the computer for two hours?
> The computer uses 4 kW (kilowatts) per hour. Electricity costs 8 cents per kW.
> 4 kW/hr × 2 hr = 8 kW
> 8 kW × 8 cents = 64 cents

1. An air conditioner uses 3 kW per hour. It costs _____ to use it for four hours.

2. The television uses 2 kW per hour. It costs _____ to watch three hours of television.

3. A microwave uses 1 kW per hour. It costs _____ to use it for half an hour.

4. The clothes dryer uses 4 kW per hour. It costs _____ to use it for two hours.

3 UNSCRAMBLE the words. Write them on the lines.

1. oofr _____

2. replfieac _____

3. mostthater _____

4. tecufa _____

5. wainshg inechma _____

6. tho retwa tnak _____

4 USE YOUR DICTIONARY. Write each verb in syllables. Circle the syllable that gets the most stress. Then practice the pronunciation with a partner.

1. carpool: (car)- pool _____

2. exercise: _____

3. insulate: _____

4. recycle: _____

5. reduce: _____

6. unplug: _____

Family Connection: Preparing for Extreme Weather

1 **MATCH** the extreme weather words with the meanings a–e.

1 flood ___c___

2 thunderstorm _____

3 tornado _____

4 hurricane _____

5 blizzard _____

a. a very bad snow storm	d. a storm with lightning and thunder
b. a storm with strong wind and rain	e. a dangerous windstorm that has a circular movement
c. ~~high levels of water~~	

2 **COMPLETE** the sentences with extreme weather words from Activity 1.

1. During a ___hurricane___, stay indoors. Stay away from windows. High winds can break them.

2. During a _____, move to high ground, such as a hill, where the water can't reach.

3. If a _____ is coming, go to the lowest floor of a building. Watch out for flying objects.

4. If you are outside during a _____, avoid lightning. Go inside or to a low place, such as a valley.

5. If you are in your car during a _____, get off the road. Exercise to keep your body warm.

3 **FIND AND MATCH.** Find the words in the sentences in Activity 2. Then match the words with their meanings.

1. _____ high winds   a. an area where the ground is higher

2. _____ hill   b. an area where the ground is lower

3. _____ objects   c. things

4. _____ valley   d. strong or fast winds

4 COMPLETE Rosa's plan for extreme weather. Use the words in the box.

blizzard	enough	far away	flashlights	movies	too	too many	too much

I just heard the weather report on the radio. Tomorrow, there's going to be a (1) _____ here in Denver. That means that we won't be able to walk outside or drive. There will be (2) _____ snow. It will be (3) _____ dangerous, so we might not go to work or to school. I'll call the school early tomorrow morning to see if it will be closed. We've had (4) _____ snow days already this year!

I'll call my boss this evening. My office is too (5) _____. Maybe I can work from home tomorrow. Is there (6) _____ food? I don't think so, so I'll go to the grocery store today and get food for two days. I'll make sure that we have enough (7) _____ and batteries. Sometimes we don't have electricity in a blizzard. The kids will have to play indoors tomorrow, so I'll rent some movies—but not too many (8) _____! We'll play some games, too. I think it'll be fun.

5 REAL-LIFE LESSON. Answer the questions.

1. Where do you get weather information—from the radio, the TV, the Internet, or another way?

   _____

2. How is your day different when it rains or snows?

   _____

   _____

3. Do you have extreme weather in your community? _____

   What kind? _____

4. If you have extreme weather, how do you prepare?

   _____

   _____

   _____

   _____

   _____

   _____

Community Connection: Temperatures in Celsius and Fahrenheit

1 READ the weather report.

---

www.weatherontheweb.net

Today's Weather

It will be cool and a little rainy here in Bay City today. The low temperature for the day will be 42° F (6° C), and the high temperature will be 47° F (8° C). Up north in Oak Ridge, conditions will be much worse. It will be much colder. The low temperature there today will be 36° F (2° C), and it might get up to 40° F (4° C) in the afternoon. It will get down to a freezing 32° F (0° C) overnight, and there is a possibility of snow. Down south in Greenville, it will be a bit warmer than it will be here today. There will be a high temperature of 59° F (15° C) in the afternoon, with a low of 52° F (11° C). Over at the beach, the temperatures will be about the same as Greenville, with a low of 53° F (11° C) and a high of 58° F (14° C), but it will be much wetter.

° = degree(s)   C = Celsius   F = Fahrenheit

---

2 CHECK ☑ *True* or *False*. Use the information in Activity 1.

	True	False
1. It will rain in Bay City today.	☐	☐
2. Greenville is the coldest place today.	☐	☐
3. Bay City is colder than Oak Ridge.	☐	☐
4. The high temperature in Bay City will be about 6° Celsius today.	☐	☐
5. 47° Fahrenheit is about 8° Celsius.	☐	☐
6. 15° Celsius is about 59° Fahrenheit.	☐	☐

3 FIND AND MATCH. Find the words in the weather report in Activity 1. Then match the words with their meanings.

_____ 1. conditions   a. reach a low temperature

_____ 2. freezing   b. high temperature

_____ 3. get down to   c. kinds of weather

_____ 4. get up to   d. very cold weather

_____ 5. high   e. reach a high temperature

_____ 6. low   f. low temperature

4 **MATCH** the Celsius temperature with the Fahrenheit temperature.

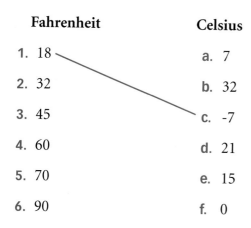

Fahrenheit	Celsius
1. 18	a. 7
2. 32	b. 32
3. 45	c. -7
4. 60	d. 21
5. 70	e. 15
6. 90	f. 0

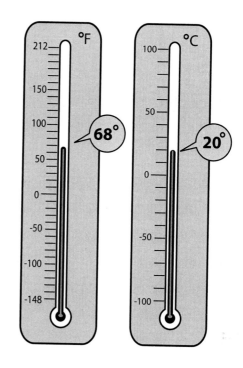

5 **MATCH** the weather conditions with correct temperatures.

1. ___c___ freezing
2. _____ cold
3. _____ cool
4. _____ warm
5. _____ hot

a. 32 degrees Celsius
b. 70 degrees Fahrenheit
c. 32 degrees Fahrenheit
d. 4 degrees Celsius
e. 50 degrees Fahrenheit

6 **REAL-LIFE LESSON.**

1. Read or listen to a weather report. Take notes.
2. Complete the chart with the weather conditions and the high and low temperatures in Fahrenheit. Use the words in the box.

cold	cool	freezing	hot	rainy	warm

Today's Weather

Conditions	Temperatures
	High _____
	Low _____

Career Connection: Making Suggestions for Improvement at Work

1 **READ** the conversation.

Office Worker:	Uh, Ms. Grant?
Manager:	Yes?
Office Worker:	I'd like to make a suggestion. We use a lot of ink. Throwing the empty ink cartridges in the garbage is bad for the environment. We should recycle our ink cartridges.
Manager:	That's an excellent idea, Nick. I agree. But how will we do this?
Office Worker:	I'll put a recycling box for empty cartridges in every office. I'll take the cartridges to the recycling center each week.
Manager:	Great! Thanks for suggesting this. Would you please send an e-mail to everyone about your idea?
Office Worker:	Sure.

Ink Cartridges

2 **WRITE.** Answer the questions.

1. What is the problem? _____

2. What is the suggestion? _____

3. What does Ms. Grant think about the suggestion? _____

4. How will Nick recycle the cartridges? _____

5. Who will tell the other employees about the plan? _____

3 **REAL-LIFE LESSON.** Think about problems in your classroom or your school. Write a suggestion for improving each one. Compare your problems and your suggestions with a partner.

Problem: _____

Suggestion: _____

Problem: _____

Suggestion: _____

Technology Connection: Tips for Writing E-mail

- Write a clear subject in the subject line. It should say what the e-mail is about.
- Keep the message short. Stay on the topic.
- Don't use ALL CAPITAL LETTERS, which can mean: "I'm angry. I'm shouting!"
- Edit your e-mail. Correct spelling and punctuation mistakes.
- Don't say anything in an e-mail that you cannot say to everyone. E-mail isn't private.

A **EDIT.** Nick's e-mail has five mistakes. Find them and correct them.

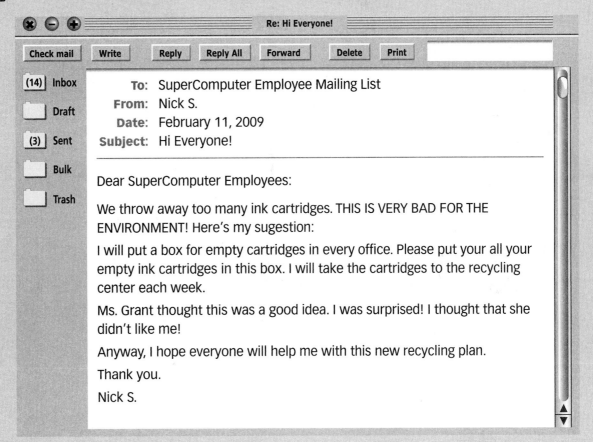

B **REAL-LIFE LESSON.** Write an e-mail to your classmates. Tell them about one of your suggestions in Activity 3 on page 100.

Practice Test

🎧 **LISTENING:** Listen to the conversation. Then listen to the question. Choose the correct answer.

1. Ⓐ Ⓑ Ⓒ   2. Ⓐ Ⓑ Ⓒ

🎧 **LISTENING:** Listen to the conversation. Then choose the correct answer.

3. What is the customer calling about?
   A. He's calling about his appliance bill.
   B. He's calling about his electricity bill.
   C. He's calling about his air conditioner bill.

4. What is the problem with the customer's bill?
   A. It's high this month.
   B. It has a mistake.
   C. It's for the wrong customer.

5. Which is correct?
   A. The customer bought a new heater.
   B. Air conditioners use a lot of electricity.
   C. The customer used more gas this month.

GRAMMAR: Choose the correct word or phrase to complete each sentence.

6. There is too ____ in our neighborhood.
   A. many cars
   B. traffic
   C. much traffic
   D. enough traffic

7. There ____ sidewalks in this town.
   A. isn't enough
   B. aren't enough
   C. not enough
   D. is enough

8. The classroom is ____ small.
   A. enough
   B. too much
   C. too
   D. not enough

(9) ____ plastic bags (10) ____ waste.

9. A. Recycle
   B. Recycles
   C. Recycled
   D. Recycling

10. A. reduce
    B. reduces
    C. reducing
    D. reduced

VOCABULARY: Choose the best word or phrase to complete the sentence.

11. There aren't enough inexpensive apartments here. There isn't enough ____.
    A. public transportation
    B. trash collection
    C. pollution
    D. affordable housing

12. The air is bad here because there's too much ____.
    A. crime
    B. pollution
    C. housing
    D. space

13. The bridge is too ____. It isn't wide enough.
   A. heavy
   B. far away
   C. dirty
   D. narrow

14. ____ your windows keeps your home warm in winter.
   A. Reusing
   B. Recycling
   C. Weatherproofing
   D. Unplugging

15. ____ your TV at night saves energy.
   A. Reducing
   B. Insulating
   C. Unplugging
   D. Reusing

READING: Read. Choose the correct answer.

City Recycling Services

The city provides recycling services once a week. Your recycling day is **WEDNESDAY**. Please put all recyclables in the blue bin. The city recycles the following items:

Paper—Newspapers, magazines, computer paper, junk mail, phone books. DO NOT include tissues, dirty food containers, or paper towels.

Food and beverage glass—Please rinse before recycling. DO NOT include light bulbs or window glass.

Plastic containers—Milk, soda, water, shampoo, and detergent bottles. DO NOT include any other kinds of plastic.

Metal—Aluminum and steel cans. DO NOT include hangers or metal containers with liquid in them.

Note: We do not recycle electronic waste such as computers, printers, and TVs.

---

16. This brochure is about ____.
   A. trash collection
   B. recycling
   C. electronic waste
   D. saving energy

17. When does the city provide recycling services?
   A. twice a week
   B. every other Wednesday
   C. once a month
   D. once a week

18. Which is a rule about recycling?
   A. Tie newspapers with string.
   B. Only recycle clear glass.
   C. Rinse glass containers.
   D. Sort your recycling.

19. Which CAN you recycle?
   A. window glass
   B. plastic shampoo bottles
   C. clothes hangers
   D. TVs

20. Which CAN'T you recycle?
   A. plastic bags
   B. phone books
   C. plastic water bottles
   D. junk mail

Lesson 1

1 COMPLETE the conversations. Write the letters of the correct questions and answers.

1. A: Have you contacted someone to help you with your taxes?

   B: _b_

2. A: Have you read about recycling? It's great for the environment

   B: _____

3. A: _____

   B: No, I haven't. But I want to try yoga.

4. A: Have you received a brochure from the employment center yet?

   B: _____

5. A: I'm going to London next week.

   B: _____

6. A: _____

   B: Yes, I have. I've registered them for the library's summer reading program.

a. Have you registered for any fitness classes at the community center?

b. ~~No, we haven't. We do our tax preparation ourselves.~~

c. Great! Have you checked out HipLondoner.com? They have a great calendar of local events.

d. Have you enrolled your kids in any programs for the summer?

e. Yes, I have. That's why I have an online subscription to the newspaper. It saves paper.

f. Yes, I got some information about career advancement yesterday.

2 COMPLETE the sentences. Use the present perfect and *yet* or *already*.

1. Ellen ___hasn't enrolled___ (not enroll) in summer school ___yet.___

2. I ___have already contacted___ (contact) somebody to help me with tax preparation.

3. Dan _____ (register) for a fitness class.

4. Ed _____ (not subscribe) to the online magazine _____.

5. I _____ (check out) the new swimming pool at the gym.

6. I _____ (not receive) a call from the employment center _____.

Lesson 2

1 **COMPLETE** the paragraph. Use the present perfect form of the verb.

> Jane and I moved to River City last month. We (1) ___'ve found___ (find) an apartment,
>
> and Jane (2) _____ (find) a job. I (3) _____ (not get)
>
> a job yet, but I (4) _____ (go) to the employment center. It has some
>
> free career development classes. Of course, I will look for a job on the Web, but we
>
> (5) _____ (not subscribed) to an Internet service yet. We
>
> (6) _____ (buy) a used car, and Jane (7) _____ (get)
>
> her driver's license. I (8) _____ (not take) the driving test yet, but I intend
>
> to next week.

2 **COMPLETE** the sentences. Write the answers in the crossword puzzle.

Across
5. I've received some information about tax preparation ____.
7. Have you ever ____ problems with your Internet service?
8. Ellen asked me to do the dishes, but I've ____ them already.

Down
1. I signed up for a subscription, but I haven't ____ a newspaper yet.
2. The online newspaper isn't very good. I've ____ a lot of mistakes in its articles.
3. Have you ____ your dog yet?
4. Dan has started a neighborhood ____ group. There's too much crime near his home.
6. I love my new yoga class. I've ____ to it three times this week.

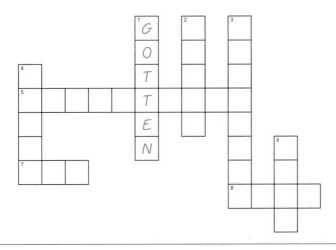

Lesson 3

1 **LISTEN** to the question. Then listen to the conversation. Listen to the question again. Fill in the circle for the correct answer.

WCD, 33

1. Ⓐ   Ⓑ   Ⓒ

2. Ⓐ   Ⓑ   Ⓒ

3. Ⓐ   Ⓑ   Ⓒ

2 **LISTEN** again to part of the conversation. Check ☑ the things that Sam has done.

WCD, 34

☐ found an apartment

☐ gotten a driver's license

☐ enrolled the children in an after-school program

☐ found a job

☐ checked out the city website

☐ found a tutor for Rob

3 **MATH.** Solve the problems. Use the percentages formula.

Percentages
To find the percentage:
1. Multiply the number by the percent. (150.00 × 50 = 7500.00)
2. Divide the answer by 100. (7500.00 ÷ 100 = 75.00)
Note: When you divide by 100, you are just moving the decimal two places to the left.

1. Your medical bill is $150. You need to pay 70%. You need to pay $ _____.

2. David's medical bill is $80. He needs to pay 50%. He needs to pay $ _____.

3. Steven needs to pay 30% of his medical bill of $60. He needs to pay $ _____.

4. My medical bill is $200. I need to pay 40%. I need to pay $ _____.

Culture and Communication: Providing Additional Information

1 **READ** the conversation.

A: Hi, Sara. It's nice to see you. What do you think of our community center?

B: It's great. I want to take some fitness classes here.

A: Good. We offer all kinds of classes. Have you ever taken a swimming class?

B: Yes, I have. In fact, I've taken many swimming classes. I love to swim!

A: Wonderful! We also have dance classes. Have you ever taken a dance class?

B: No, I haven't, but I've taken singing lessons.

A: Really! We also have art classes. Have you taken any art classes?

B: Yes, I have. In fact, I've taught art classes to seniors.

A: Great! Maybe you can work here, too!

Culture Tip

When someone asks you a question about your experience, it's okay to answer the question and give additional information.

It's also a good idea to express confidence in yourself; be positive about your experience and skills.

Useful Expressions

Yes, I have. I've also…	Yes, I have. For example, I've…
Yes, I have. In fact, I've…	No, I haven't, but I've…

---

2 **WRITE** answers to the questions about Sara.

1. What has Sara done? _____

2. What hasn't Sara done? _____

3. What information does Sara add? _____

4. Why might Sara add information about herself? _____

3 **PRACTICE.** Talk to a partner. Student A asks a question. Student B answers and provides additional information. Use the expressions above. Then exchange roles.

1. Have you ever helped out at a senior center?
2. Have you checked out the library in your town?
3. Have you ever taken a career advancement class?
4. Have you ever taken a class at a community center?
5. Have you ever taken a fitness class?
6. Have you checked out the city website?

Lesson 4

1 **WRITE** the phrases. Use the words in the box.

| diabetic | on strike | retired | ~~Internet service down~~ | out of work | without electricity |

1. Internet service down

2. _____

3. _____

4. _____

5. _____

6. _____

2 **MATCH** the questions with the answers. Write the letters.

_c_ 1. How long have you been out of work?

____ 2. How long has she been diabetic?

____ 3. How long has Dan been retired?

____ 4. How long have they been without electricity?

____ 5. How long have they been on strike?

____ 6. How long has your Internet service been down?

a. He's been retired for two years.

b. She's had diabetes for a year.

c. ~~Since May. I lost my job on May 1.~~

d. Since yesterday, and I need to go online!

e. The electricity has been out since yesterday.

f. Since Friday. That's when the strike started.

Lesson 5

1 **PRACTICE.** Work with a partner. Student A reads a sentence aloud. Student B says "simple past" or "past perfect." Circle the verb. Then exchange roles.

1. They 've registered for classes.

2. She's had Internet service for a week.

3. Ellen had diabetes for two years.

4. We bought a new car.

5. I received the tickets.

6. We've enrolled in classes already.

2 **WRITE** questions using the present perfect.

1. How long / you / be / student?

   How long have you been a student?

2. How long / you / live / this city?

   _____

3. How long / you / go / this school?

   _____

4. How long / you / study / English?

   _____

5. How long / you / drive / car?

   _____

3 **WRITE** four more questions. Use the present perfect with *How long*. Then ask and answer questions from Activities 2 and 3 with your partner.

Example: *How long have you been a waiter?*

4 **USE YOUR DICTIONARY.** Find the correct forms to complete the chart.

Noun	Verb
	assist
preparation	
	register
	retire
subscription	subscribe

Family Connection: Getting Information by Phone

1 WRITE. How do you get phone numbers? Check ☑ the ways. Then write another way.

- ☐ online
- ☐ in the phone book
- ☐ by calling directory assistance (4-1-1)
- ☐ by asking a friend
- ☐ other: _____

2 READ the conversation.

> *Bob:* Sara, let's enroll the children in swimming classes.
>
> *Sara:* Great idea. How about at the community center? Do you have the schedule?
>
> *Bob:* No. Let's call and ask for a calendar of events. What's their number?
>
> *Sara:* I don't know. Let's try directory assistance.
>
> *Bob:* Good idea. I'm going to call right now. Okay. Um, let's see... 4-1-1...
>
> *Operator:* Directory assistance. What city, please?
>
> *Bob:* Greenville.
>
> *Operator:* What listing, please?
>
> *Bob:* I'd like the phone number for the community center.
>
> *Operator:* Is that the Greenville Community Center on Park Street?
>
> *Bob:* That's it.
>
> *Recording:* The number is 213-555-3469. Press "1" to be connected immediately. Extra charges may apply.
>
> *Bob:* Here's the number. Let's dial it ourselves. I don't want to pay the extra money.
>
> *Sara:* Good idea.

3 CHECK ☑ *True* or *False*. Then correct the false statements. Write the corrected sentences in your notebook.

	True	False
1. Bob wants to enroll the children in a reading program.	☐	☐
2. Sara knows the phone number of the community center.	☐	☐
3. The community center is on Park Street.	☐	☐
4. Bob calls 911 to get the community center phone number.	☐	☐
5. The operator asks Bob for an address.	☐	☐
6. It costs extra money if the phone company makes the call for you.	☐	☐

4 **FIND AND MATCH.** Find the words and phrases in the conversation in Activity 2. Then match them with their meanings.

_____ 1. charges may apply

_____ 2. directory assistance

_____ 3. listing

_____ 4. be connected

a. you might have to pay money

b. a person or company that has a phone number

c. get in contact with on the phone

d. a service that gives callers phone numbers

5 **PRACTICE.** Read the example and the situations. Have conversations with a partner. Student A needs a phone number. Student B is the 411 operator. Then switch roles.

Example:

B: Directory assistance. What city and listing, please?

A: I need the number for Dr. Yee in Greenville.

B: There's a Dr. Yee on Oak Street.

A: That's it.

B: The number is 213-555-7869.

Situations

1. Student A: You need the number for the *Brownsville Times* newspaper in Brownsville. You don't know the street.

   Student B: It's 213-555-8392. It's on Peach Street.

2. Student A: You need the number of Happy Days Summer Camp on Cherry Street in Greenville.

   Student B: It's 213-555-6794.

3. Student A: You need the number of a dentist on May Street in Bay City. You can't remember the name. The number is 320-555-3845.

   Student B: Her name is Dr. Arons.

6 **REAL-LIFE LESSON.** Ask a friend or family member to recommend the names of the following community services in your area. Get the phone numbers and write them below. Next, call and ask for the address.

Community Service	Name	Address	Phone Number
community center			
fitness classes			
employment center			
doctor			
dentist			
other/your choice			

Community Connection: Using Postal Services

1 **READ** the information from the United States Postal Service website.

domestic = in the United States	international = outside the United States

United States Postal Service — Mailing Services

Service	Price	Delivery Time
Domestic		
First-Class Mail®	$0.41 and up	2-3 Days
Priority Mail® (Includes extra services)	$4.60 and up	2-3 Days
Express Mail®	$16.25 and up	Next Day
International		
First-Class Mail International®	$0.69 and up	6-10 Days
Priority Mail® International (Includes extra services)	$16.00 and up	6-10 Days
Express Mail International®	$22.00 and up	3-5 Days

First-Class Letters First-class letters include postcards, letters, and large envelopes. They can weigh up to 13 ounces. For heavier items, use Priority Mail®.

First-Class Packages First-class packages include boxes and thick envelopes. They can weigh up to 13 ounces. For heavier items, use Priority Mail®.

2 **COMPLETE** the sentences about U.S. postal services.

1. The fastest and most expensive way to send a letter in the U.S. is by _____.

2. The least expensive way to send a letter is by _____.

3. If a letter weighs 12 ounces, you can send it by _____.

4. If a package weighs one pound, you should send it by _____.

5. To send a package from the U.S. to Mexico in four days, you will pay at least _____.

3 **READ** about additional postal services on the United States Postal Service website.

> **Additional Services**
>
> **Registered Mail™** is for sending items that are very expensive or that you cannot replace. **Registered Mail™** includes insurance if your letter or package is lost or damaged. It also gives you the date and time of delivery. You can combine Registered Mail™ with other postal services:
>
> **Signature Confirmation™** gives you the date and time of delivery and the signature of the person who accepts it.
>
> **Return receipt** includes a receipt. The receipt shows the signature of the person who accepted the item. It gives you the delivery address, too. You can receive a receipt by mail or by e-mail.

4 **FIND AND MATCH.** Find the words in the information above. Then match the words with their meanings.

____ 1. accepted

____ 2. confirmation

____ 3. damaged

____ 4. insurance

____ 5. time of delivery

a. a notice that something has happened

b. money to pay for an accident

c. time of arrival

d. received

e. hurt; broken

5 **COMPLETE** the sentences. Write the best service for the situation. More than one answer is possible.

1. Lara is mailing an expensive present to her grandmother. She should probably use _____.

2. Today is the last day to mail tax forms. Bob needs to prove that he mailed his forms today. He also wants to know that someone has received them. Bob should probably _____.

3. Dan mailed some important work to his company. The company can't find it. Dan's not worried. He knows that the company received it. He even knows who received it because he paid for _____.

6 **REAL-LIFE LESSON.** Find answers to the following questions.

1. Where is the post office in your community? _____

   What hours is it open? _____

2. Are there other services in your community for sending letters or packages? _____

   If yes, what are they? _____

   How are they different from what the post office offers? _____

Career Connection: Interpreting Job Listings

1 **READ** the job ads at a community center.

Community Center Café
The Community Center Café is looking for a part-time assistant manager. Must have experience. Spanish-speaker preferred. The assistant manager helps the manager, makes work schedules, and supervises employees.

The Bayview Community Center is growing!
We need a construction worker. The construction worker will help build our new fitness center. You must have a driver's license and two years' experience. Apply online.

Art Teacher
The community center manager is looking for a part-time art teacher. Must have experience with children. Please apply in person Monday–Friday, 10:00 A.M.–4:00 P.M.

Volunteer drivers needed!
The Bayview Community Center needs van drivers to help seniors get to the center. No experience necessary. We will train you. Must have a good driving record. Apply online.

2 **WRITE.** Read about the people. Write answers to the questions.

1. *Lucy:* I graduated from college last June. During college, I volunteered at a community center. I worked with children there. I haven't taught art to children, but I've taught art to adults.

   What's the best job for Lucy? _____

   Why? _____

2. *Rob:* My father is a carpenter. I've helped him build houses for five years, but I don't have a driver's license yet.

   Can Rob apply for the construction job? _____

   Why or why not? _____

3. *Raul:* I worked at Lina's Café for 5 years. I haven't made work schedules, but I've supervised employees. I speak Spanish fluently.

   What job can Raul probably get? _____

   Why? _____

4. *Sara:* I like to help out in the community. I like working with senior citizens. I've never driven a van, but I'd like to learn.

   What's the best job for Sara? _____

   Why? _____

Technology Connection: Filling Out an Online Job Application

- Have all your information ready
- Print the application. Fill it out by hand. Proofread it carefully.
- Complete the online application. Copy from your printed and filled-out application.
- Print out your completed application. Proofread it again. Correct any mistakes online.
- Then click Submit.

A **READ** Sara's online job application. Find and circle Sara's social security number, the number of years she went to school, and the position she is applying for.

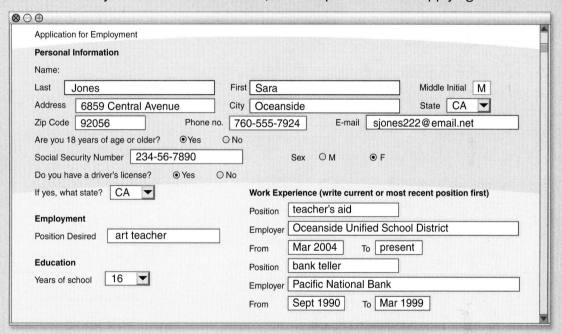

B **COMPLETE** the online job application for yourself. Edit it carefully.

Practice Test

LISTENING: Listen to the question. Then listen to the conversation. Listen to the question again. Choose the correct answer.

1. (A)   (B)   (C)   2. (A)   (B)   (C)

LISTENING: Listen to the conversation. Then choose the correct answer.

3. What type of agency is the man calling?
   A. a dental clinic
   B. an eye clinic
   C. a health insurance office

4. What is the man's yearly income?
   A. $13,000
   B. $30,000
   C. $33,000

5. How much will the man have to pay for an eye exam?
   A. $34.00
   B. $40.00
   C. $85.00

GRAMMAR: Choose the correct word or phrase to complete each sentence.

Tony (6) ____ already (7) ____ the brochure.

6. A. have
   B. had
   C. having
   D. has

7. A. receives
   B. receive
   C. received
   D. receiving

8. Have you ____ a car yet?
   A. buy
   B. bought
   C. buying
   D. buys

9. How long have you ____?
   A. being unemployed
   B. been unemployed
   C. be unemployed
   D. unemployed

10. I have been unemployed for ____.
    A. last year
    B. 2010
    C. one year
    D. this year

VOCABULARY: Choose the best word or phrase to complete the sentence.

11. I need some exercise. I'm going to take a ____ class.
    A. career advancement
    B. fitness
    C. tax preparation
    D. local events

12. I've already ____ to the local newspaper. It comes every morning.
    A. registered
    B. checked out
    C. received
    D. subscribed

13. Can you help me? I need tax preparation ____.
    A. license
    B. assistance
    C. fitness classes
    D. subscriptions

14. The bus drivers aren't working. They're ____.
    A. without electricity
    B. on strike
    C. down
    D. on hold

15. I called the phone company at 11:00 A.M. I've been ____ for an hour!
    A. on strike
    B. on time
    C. on board
    D. on hold

READING: Read. Choose the correct answer.

A Talk with River City's Volunteer of the Month: Ana Santos

Jim: Tell me about yourself, Ana.

Ana: Well, I was born in Mexico, but I have lived in the United States since 1985. I have three children, and I am a full-time science teacher at River City Community College.

Jim: And how long have you been a community volunteer?

Ana: I've been a community volunteer for over 15 years.

Jim: What organizations are you interested in?

Ana: I support many organizations. I'm especially interested in environmental causes. I want a cleaner River City. For example, in 2008, I started a campus recycling program.

Jim: What other things have you done here in River City?

Ana: I've also volunteered for the Clean Water Organization. I've worked very hard to clean up our river.

Jim: And today, we can swim in the river, thanks to Ana.

---

16. Where was Ana born?
    A. the United States
    B. River City
    C. Mexico
    D. Santa Ana

17. Where is Ana's job?
    A. at a college
    B. at a recycling company
    C. at a garbage collection company
    D. at the Clean Water Organization

18. How long has Ana been a volunteer?
    A. for 15 years
    B. since 1985
    C. for three years
    D. since 2008

19. What kind of organizations does Ana volunteer for?
    A. science
    B. environmental
    C. children's
    D. sports

20. An example of an environmental cause is
    A. a family
    B. a campus recycling program
    C. a teaching career
    D. a community

Lesson 1

1 COMPLETE the conversations with the words and phrases in the box.

baking	organizing work tools	translating documents
handing out flyers	picking tomatoes	~~weeding~~

1. *A:* Our garden doesn't look very good.

   B: No, Rob hasn't been _____*weeding*_____ today.

2. *A:* Our garage looks very neat!

   B: Yes, Pete has been _____. Now we can find everything!

3. *A:* I've been _____ all morning. What are we going to do with them?

   B: I'll make spaghetti with tomato sauce for dinner.

4. *A:* What's that nice smell?

   B: I've been _____ cookies.

5. *A:* Sue is looking for her lost dog. What has she been doing?

   B: She's been _____ all day.

6. *A:* Jane is working in her office with a lot of dictionaries. What has she been doing?

   B: She's been _____ all day.

2 COMPLETE the the sentences. Use the present perfect continuous of the verbs in the box.

bake	(not) feel	hand out	organize	translate	weed

1. Mike _____*has not been feeling*_____ well. He needs to see a doctor.

2. I smell something delicious. _____ you _____ cookies?

3. The garage looks clean and neat. Ed _____ all of our tools.

4. My jeans are very dirty! I _____ in the garden all morning.

5. Everyone knows about the town meeting now. Ella _____ flyers.

6. Look! These reports are in Spanish and English. _____ they _____

   _____ these documents?

Lesson 2

1 COMPLETE the paragraph. Use the present perfect continuous of the verbs in the box.

fix	organize	paint	plant	weed	~~work~~

My sister Ella and I have been busy lately. We (1) _____have been working_____ around the house a lot because we want to sell it. Ella (2) _____ the walls. I (3) _____ all the boxes in the garage because it was really messy. Ella (4) _____ the garden because a lot of weeds have been growing recently. Both of us (5) _____ a lot of bright flowers. My back aches because I (6) _____ some other things around the house, too.

2 UNSCRAMBLE the words. Write them on the lines. Then match the number of each word with a picture below.

1. remmah _____hammer_____
2. levhos _____
3. hcnrew _____
4. dalder _____
5. snail _____
6. froktciph _____

a. _____   b. _____   c. _____   d. ___1___   e. _____

f. _____

Lesson 3

1 LISTEN. Write *has* or *hasn't* under the pictures.

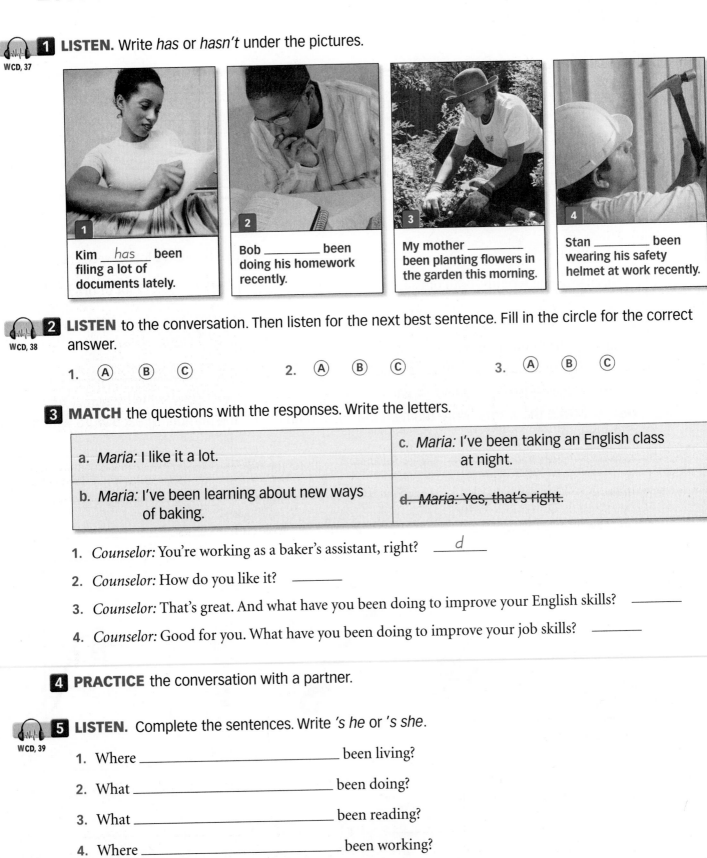

1 Kim __has__ been filing a lot of documents lately.

2 Bob _____ been doing his homework recently.

3 My mother _____ been planting flowers in the garden this morning.

4 Stan _____ been wearing his safety helmet at work recently.

2 LISTEN to the conversation. Then listen for the next best sentence. Fill in the circle for the correct answer.

1. Ⓐ Ⓑ Ⓒ   2. Ⓐ Ⓑ Ⓒ   3. Ⓐ Ⓑ Ⓒ

3 MATCH the questions with the responses. Write the letters.

a. *Maria:* I like it a lot.	**c.** *Maria:* I've been taking an English class at night.
b. *Maria:* I've been learning about new ways of baking.	**d.** *Maria:* Yes, that's right.

1. *Counselor:* You're working as a baker's assistant, right? ___d___

2. *Counselor:* How do you like it? _____

3. *Counselor:* That's great. And what have you been doing to improve your English skills? _____

4. *Counselor:* Good for you. What have you been doing to improve your job skills? _____

4 PRACTICE the conversation with a partner.

5 LISTEN. Complete the sentences. Write *'s he* or *'s she*.

1. Where _____ been living?

2. What _____ been doing?

3. What _____ been reading?

4. Where _____ been working?

5. What _____ been making?

120 | Unit 9

Culture and Communication: Asking for and Giving Advice

Culture Tip
In the United States, people often work at improving career skills throughout their lives. It is common to ask for career advice. In fact, people often pay for career advice from career counselors, and they may take career advancement classes.

Useful Expressions	
Asking for Advice	**Giving Advice**
What else can I do...?	Why don't you...?
What else do you suggest I do...?	How about...?
Do you have any suggestions for me?	What about...?
Can you give me some advice?	Have you thought about...?
	I suggest that you...

1 **READ** the conversations.

1

A: I've been working as a front desk clerk for two years. I'd like to be a manager. What can I do to improve my skills?

B: I suggest that you take a hotel management class at the community college.

A: Thanks. I'll look into that.

2

A: I've been translating documents at this company for five years. I'd like to be a writer. What do you suggest I do to improve my skills?

B: Have you thought about taking a business writing class?

A: Great idea! Thanks.

2 **WRITE** answers to the questions about Activity 1.

1. In Conversation 1, why does the young woman ask for advice?

_____

   Underline the man's suggestion.

2. In Conversation 2, why does the young man ask for advice?

_____

   Underline the woman's suggestion.

3 **PRACTICE.** Read the situations. Talk with a partner. Ask for and give advice. Use the Useful Expressions. Then exchange roles.

1. You have been working as an office assistant for two years. You want to improve your skills.
2. You have been studying English for three years. You want to improve your skills.
3. You've been working at a hotel for many years. You want to become a manager.

Lesson 4

1 COMPLETE the phrases. Use the words in the box. Use each word once.

coaching	designing	~~raising~~
creating	directing	signing

1

_____raising_____ money

2

_____ soccer

3

_____ homes

4

_____ movies

5

_____ websites

6

_____ books

2 COMPLETE the sentences. Use present perfect and present perfect continuous of the verbs in Activity 1.

1. Mary and Tony ____*have been raising*____ money for the homeless shelter for two months. They ____*have raised*____ over $3,000.

2. Dave _____ five different soccer teams. He _____ soccer since 2003.

3. They _____ over 50 homes. They _____ homes for 20 years.

4. Tony _____ films since 2001. He _____ five films.

5. Rani _____ websites since she was 30. She _____ over 20 sites.

6. Sandy _____ books since this morning. She _____ about 100 books.

Lesson 5

1 **MATH.** Read the problem. Answer the questions.

You are the manager at a translation company. You need an employee for an important job, but everyone is busy. Calculate the time each employee needs to complete their job.

1. Stella has to translate three documents. It takes four hours to translate each document. She's been translating documents for six hours. _____

2. Evan has to answer 24 e-mails. It takes five minutes to answer each e-mail. He's been answering e-mails for 20 minutes. _____

3. Angela has to make 15 phone calls. It takes 10 minutes to complete each phone call. She's been making phone calls for two hours. _____

Which employee will finish the job first? _____

2 **COMPLETE** the story about Anna. Use the present perfect continuous or the present perfect form of the verbs.

Anna started playing the violin when she was eight years old. She (1) _has been playing_ (play) for ten years. Anna's concerts are very popular. She (2) _____ (have) ten concerts this year. Half of the money from her concerts goes to a homeless shelter. Anna (3) _____ (raised) more than $2,000 for the homeless. She also sells a lot of CDs. She (4) _____ (sell) CDs for five years. Anna (5) _____ (sell) more than 1,000 CDs. She often signs her CDs at music stores. She (6) _____ (sign) more than 200 CDs.

3 **USE YOUR DICTIONARY.** Use the words in the box to answer the questions.

sign	create	raise	design	direct

1. Which verbs have more than one syllable? _____

2. Which verbs have two vowels together? _____
   Practice the pronunciation with a partner.

3. Write the verbs in alphabetical order. _____

Family Connection: Conducting Information Interviews

1 WRITE. What are some ways to find out about different careers? Check ☑ the ways. Write two new ways.

- ☐ ask my family
- ☐ read books and articles
- ☐ take a class
- ☐ do Internet research
- ☐ talk to friends

another way: _____

another way: _____

2 READ the article about information interviews.

Information Interviews

1   An information interview is a way to get information about a career. In an information interview, you talk to people who have the job you want. You find out how they got it.

2   An information interview can help you to choose a career goal. It can also help you find the career path for that goal. A career path can be the courses you need to take or the experience you need to have. An information interview also is a way to network. Networking is getting to know people who can help you. These contacts—people who know you—might help you to get a job later on.

3   Who should you interview? Ask your family. Ask everyone you know. Then call or write a letter to the person and ask for an information interview. Don't be shy. Most people like to give advice—but don't ask for a job! Remember, you are just asking for an information interview— an appointment to get information.

4   Before you go on the interview, prepare a list of questions that you want to ask. These might include:

- How long have you been working here?
- What job did you have before?
- What did you study in school?
- How did you train for this job?
- What are your responsibilities?

5   During your interview, be confident. Make eye contact. Always ask the person for the name of another person to interview later. This will help you add to your network of contacts. When the interview is over, thank the person for being so helpful.

3 (CIRCLE) the correct number.

Which paragraph has…

1.	a definition of information interview?	1	2	3	4	5
2.	reasons to conduct an information interview?	1	2	3	4	5
3.	an explanation of how to prepare for an information interview?	1	2	3	4	5
4.	examples of questions to ask in an information interview?	1	2	3	4	5
5.	examples of ways to find people to interview?	1	2	3	4	5

4 **FIND AND MATCH.** Find the words in the article. Then match the words with their meanings.

1. _____ career path
2. _____ contacts
3. _____ information interview
4. _____ network (noun)
5. _____ network (verb)

a. get to know people who can help you
b. things you need to do to get a career
c. a group of people who can help you
d. people who know you
e. getting information about jobs by talking to people

5 **WRITE.** Think of a job or a company that you are interested in. Write a list of questions for an information interview.

Job title: _____   Company: _____

1. _____
2. _____
3. _____
4. _____

6 **REAL-LIFE LESSON.** Practice an information interview with a friend or family member. Use these questions or your own.

- Can you give me some advice?
- How long have you worked at _____?
- What job did you have before?
- What did you study in school? *or* How did you train for this job?
- What are your duties?
- Is there anyone else you think I should talk to?
- Your questions: _____
  _____
  _____

Community Connection: Writing a Thank You Note

1 **READ** the thank you note for an information interview.

Mark Malone
4257 Pine Street
Chula Vista, CA 91910

Dear Mr. Malone:

Thank for very much for giving me the opportunity for an information interview with you. I liked talking with you and learning more about working as a translator.

Your advice is very valuable to me. In addition to taking more classes, you also suggested that I spend time in Latin America. You said: "When you translate, knowing the culture is as important as knowing the language." This is very good advice, and I won't forget it.

Thank you for offering to introduce me to other translators. I have been building a network of contacts in the translation field, and I know that these people will be very important to me.

Sincerely,

Yolanda Sanchez

Yolanda Sanchez

2 **WRITE** answers to the questions about the letter.

1. How many times does Yolanda say thank you? _____

2. In which paragraph does Yolanda first say thank you? _____

3. In which paragraph does Yolanda say the name of the job she is interested in? _____

4. What advice did Mr. Malone give to Yolanda? In which paragraph does she talk about his advice?

    _____

5. How else did Mr. Malone help Yolanda? In which paragraph does she talk about this?

    _____

3 **FIND AND MATCH.** Find the words in the letter. Then match the words with the meanings.

_____ 1. field   a. worth a lot

_____ 2. opportunity   b. suggesting

_____ 3. offering   c. area of work

_____ 4. valuable   d. possibility

4 READ Ted's thank you letter again. Ted followed some of the tips, but not all of them. Circle *Yes* or *No*.

Did Ted…

1. say thank you in the first paragraph?   Yes   No

2. repeat the person's advice or other important information from the interview?   Yes   No

3. ask for more advice?   Yes   No

4. write a formal letter?   Yes   No

5. proofread his letter?   Yes   No

Tips

Writing an Information Interview Thank You Letter

- Say thank you in the first paragraph.
- Repeat important advice or information that the person said in the interview.
- Ask for more advice.
- Be formal. Address the person with "Dear," Mr./Ms./Mrs., and the last name. Sign with "Sincerely" and your first and last name.
- Proofread your letter before you send it.

5 EDIT Ted's letter. Correct these mistakes he made.

- two spelling mistakes
- one punctuation mistake
- one capitalization mistake
- one grammar mistake

Tina Yu
4257 Pine Street
Costa Verde, CA 92122

Hey Ms. Yu,

It was great to see you yesterday. I really enjoyed talking with you You have a very cool office. I especially like the surfing posters on your wall.

I have been thinking about a hotel carear. After I talked with you, I have definitely decide that I want to go into the hotel business. thanks for your offer to introduce me to other people in the feild. I think that will help me a lot.

If you think of anybody else I should talk to, please let me know.

Take care,

Ted

---

6 REAL-LIFE LESSON. Write a thank you letter to the friend or family member you interviewed for Activity 6 on page 125. Use the checklist above and proofread it. Then have a classmate read your letter. Make changes if necessary. Then send your letter.

Career Connection: Asking for References and Letters of Recommendation

1 **READ** about Pete and Lara.

> Pete is applying for a job at an organization. He needs a letter of recommendation. A letter of recommendation is a letter from a person who knows you and your work. Employers like to receive letters of recommendation in the mail directly from the letter writer. Pete has been volunteering at the community center, so he asked the manager there to write a letter of recommendation. He asked the manager to send the letter directly to the organization. The community center manager likes Pete and thinks he is a good worker.
>
> Lara has been looking for a new job. She just had an interview. Now she needs two references. A reference is a person who knows you and your work. Employers call references on the phone and ask them questions about you. Lara asked her old boss and one of her teachers to be her references. They both know her well and they think she is a hard worker. They are happy to help her, so Lara will give the interviewer their phone numbers.

Tips
Asking for References and Letters of Recommendation
• Ask someone who will say good things about your work.
• Don't ask a relative.
• Ask for a letter of recommendation at least a week before you need it.
• Don't write your own letter of recommendation.
• For references, make sure that you give the correct phone number.
• Tell your references that someone might call them and ask questions about you.

2 <u>UNDERLINE</u> the words to complete the sentences.

1. Pete needs a **letter of recommendation / reference**.

2. Employers call a **reference / letter of recommendation**.

3. Employers want to receive **references / letters of recommendation** in the mail.

4. Lara's old boss is **happy / unhappy** to help.

5. You should ask for a letter of recommendation at least a **day / week** before you need it.

6. It **is / is not** necessary to tell references that someone will call them.

7. It **is / is not** a good idea to ask your mother to write you a letter of recommendation.

8. You **should / should not** write your own letter of recommendation.

 3 **WRITE.** Who knows your work? Make a list of at least three people you can ask for a reference or a letter of recommendation.

Technology Connection: ATM Safety

A **READ** about ATM safety.

ATM Safety Tips
There are a lot of things that you can do to be safe while using an ATM—an automatic teller machine. Here are some recommendations from safety experts: • Memorize your PIN—your personal identification number.   • Don't use your birthday, phone number, or address as a PIN.   • Keep your ATM card in your purse or wallet. Get it out before you go to the ATM.   • Stand directly in front of the ATM keypad when you enter your PIN. Don't let anyone see what you enter.   • Don't count your money at the ATM. Put it away and leave quickly.

B **WRITE.** Look at the picture. Match the words and the letters.

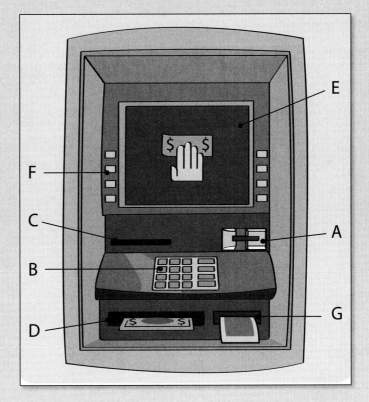

_____ 1. cash dispenser

_____ 2. deposit slot

_____ 3. display screen

_____ 4. insert your card here

_____ 5. keypad

_____ 6. receipt printer

_____ 7. screen buttons

Practice Test

LISTENING: Listen to the conversation. Then listen for the next best sentence. Choose the correct answer.

WCD, 40

1. (A)   (B)   (C)

2. (A)   (B)   (C)

LISTENING: Listen to the conversation. Then choose the correct answer.

WCD, 41

3. Who is Max?

   A. a worker

   B. a teacher

   C. a student

4. What is Ms. Sanders doing?

   A. giving advice

   B. complaining

   C. asking for help

5. What does Ms. Sanders say?

   A. Read the newspaper on weekends.

   B. Read the newspaper every day.

   C Watch the news every day.

GRAMMAR: Choose the correct word or phrase to complete each sentence.

Deb (6) _____ been (7) _____ the garden all day.

6. A. have

   B. is

   C. was

   D. has

7. A. weeding

   B. weeds

   C. weeded

   D. weed

8. Have you been _____ well lately?

   A. feel

   B. felt

   C. feels

   D. feeling

9. Where _____ he been working lately?

   A. has

   B. have

   C. had

   D. having

10. She _____ e-mail five times today.

    A. has been checking

    B. checking

    C. has checked

    D. check

VOCABULARY: Choose the best word or phrase to complete the sentence.

11. Mario likes to cook. He's been _____ cookies all day.

    A. baking

    B. designing

    C. picking

    D. doing

12. Mark understands both English and Chinese. He has been _____ documents for ten years.

    A. organizing

    B. designing

    C. directing

    D. translating

130 | Unit 9

13. Marta's a writer. She's been ____ her books at bookstores all week.

    A. signing

    B. creating

    C. directing

    D. designing

14. Bob likes to volunteer. He's been ____ money for organizations since 2002.

    A. winning

    B. raising

    C. handing out

    D. organizing

15. Joe is going to weed the garden. He needs a ____.

    A. nails

    B. pitchfork

    C. hammer

    D. paintbrush

READING: Read. Choose the correct answer.

Case Study: Ray

Ray has been a waiter for three years. He likes his job because he enjoys serving customers and the pay is good, but he would like to become a chef. He's interested in food preparation and he has been taking cooking classes at the community college. He studies recipes and cookbooks, and he reads the food section of the newspaper every Wednesday. He also talks to the chef about ingredients and menu planning. Last week, the manager at the restaurant offered Ray the opportunity to assist the chef.

---

16. What is the article about?

    A. wanting to change jobs at a restaurant

    B. becoming a waiter

    C. becoming a manager

    D. taking cooking classes

17. What is Ray's job?

    A. He's a chef.

    B. He's a manager.

    C. He's a cooking teacher.

    D. He's a waiter.

18. What job would Ray like to have?

    A. chef

    B. manager

    C. waiter

    D. writer

19. What opportunity did Ray get?

    A. the opportunity to take classes at the community college

    B. the opportunity to plan menus

    C. the opportunity to be a manager

    D. the opportunity to assist the chef

20. Which statement is an inference?

    A. Ray has taken cooking classes.

    B. Ray likes to learn about food and cooking.

    C. Ray likes his job.

    D. Ray reads the food section of the newspaper.

UNIT **10** Solving Problems

Lesson 1

1 **COMPLETE** the sentences. Use the words in the box.

fax machine	laptop	photocopier runs out	jams	~~outside call~~	scanner

1 How do I make an ___outside___ ___call___?

2 The _____ won't start. What should I do?

3 How do I save a file on this _____?

4 If you want to use the _____ _____, dial the **fax number**

5 What do I do if the _____ _____ of paper?

6 What do I do if paper _____ in the printer?

2 **MATCH** the phrases to make complete sentences. Write the letters.

1. If paper gets stuck in the printer, ___c___
2. If you want to make an outside call, _____
3. If he wants to save a file, _____
4. If the scanner doesn't start, _____
5. If the photocopier runs out of paper, _____
6. If you need to use the fax machine, _____

a. he should click "Save."
b. you should press nine first.
c. ~~you should turn off the power.~~
d. they should make sure the power is on.
e. you should dial the fax number first.
f. we should put more paper in it.

Lesson 2

1 **COMPLETE** the chart. Write the nouns in the correct column.

aspirin	cold pack	fire alarm	smoke detector
bandages	emergency exit	flashlight	~~warning sign~~

Safety Equipment in a Building	Items in a First Aid Kit
warning sign	

2 **FIND** the words from Activity 1. (Circle) them. Words can be up and down, across, or diagonal. They can be forward or backward.

A	S	R	W	C	O	L	D	P	A	C	K	Y	E	S	B
U	S	I	W	F	F	P	S	Y	T	Y	W	H	W	D	A
M	U	P	F	I	D	I	Z	E	E	H	Q	N	Q	Y	N
S	M	S	I	K	S	U	W	M	W	N	Q	R	S	H	D
C	L	F	R	R	W	Y	Q	E	S	U	O	F	N	N	A
W	S	X	E	O	I	H	Y	R	V	T	A	L	G	U	G
Y	V	G	A	L	A	N	U	G	C	J	Z	A	I	K	E
F	I	Q	L	P	A	R	K	E	Y	M	Z	S	S	T	S
K	U	Z	A	L	Z	E	T	N	U	I	X	H	G	G	Y
D	S	I	R	K	C	E	O	C	R	K	C	L	N	F	H
Y	V	K	M	H	D	W	K	Y	D	L	V	I	I	E	U
K	J	O	S	E	Y	S	P	E	X	O	F	G	N	C	J
S	P	Y	K	S	U	F	L	X	F	P	G	H	R	X	I
I	U	O	C	E	J	F	R	I	S	T	T	T	A	Z	K
D	M	U	A	F	K	G	E	T	F	R	E	U	W	C	L
S	D	I	C	C	L	T	D	D	X	E	S	J	C	X	M

Lesson 3

 1 LISTEN. Draw a line from the words to the correct number on the cell phone keypad.

WCD, 42

play

save

delete

leave new message

directory of employees

hear again

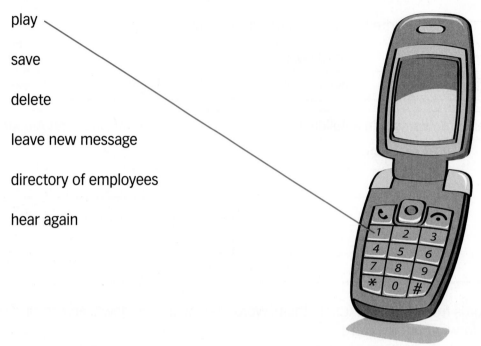

 2 LISTEN to the conversation. Then listen to the question. Fill in the circle for the correct answer.

WCD, 43

1. Ⓐ Ⓑ Ⓒ

2. Ⓐ Ⓑ Ⓒ

3. Ⓐ Ⓑ Ⓒ

 3 LISTEN. Check ☑ the correct box.

WCD, 44

1. ☐ *Yes/No* Question   ☐ *Wh-* Question

2. ☐ *Yes/No* Question   ☐ *Wh-* Question

3. ☐ *Yes/No* Question   ☐ *Wh-* Question

4. ☐ *Yes/No* Question   ☐ *Wh-* Question

4 PRACTICE saying the questions with a partner.

1. If the paper gets stuck, do I turn off the power?

2. If I want to save a file, should I click "Save"?

3. If the photocopier runs out of paper, what should I do?

4. If I want to make a call, do I press 9?

Culture and Communication: Taking Phone Messages

1 **READ** the conversation. Then read the message. Answer the questions.

A: Hello?
B: Hi. This is Rick Green. Is Jane Smith there?
A: No, she isn't. Can I take a message?
B: Yes. Please tell her to call me.
A: Sure. What's your number?
B: My number is 213-555-7980.

Message

Date/Time: ___June 3___ ___6:00 p.m.___

To: ___Jane Smith___

From: ___Rick Green___

Phone number: ___213-555-7980___

Message: ___Call him.___

_____

_____

_____

_____

1. Who called? _____

2. Who is the message for? _____

3. What is the caller's phone number? _____

4. What is the message? _____

2 **LISTEN.** Listen to the conversation. Write the caller's message.

WCD, 45

Message

Date/Time: _____

To: _____

From: _____

Phone number: _____

Message: _____

_____

_____

Lesson 4

1 MATCH the pictures with the sentences. Write the letters.

1. _d_	2. ____	3. ____
4. ____	5. ____	6. ____

a. If I invest money now, I'll have enough money to retire.

b. I don't like to commute so far to work.

c. If I don't keep fit, I'll gain weight.

d. ~~I'm going to get home early tonight!~~

e. I like to work the morning shift.

f. I'll get a better job if I improve my computer skills.

2 COMPLETE the sentences. Use the correct form of the verbs.

1. If I _____don't keep fit_____ (not keep fit), I _____will gain_____ (gain) weight.

2. If I _____ (invest) money every month, I _____ (retire) in ten years.

3. What _____ you _____ (do) if you _____ (not find) a job?

4. If you _____ (work) more hours, _____ you _____ (have) time to study?

5. If Dan _____ (study) a lot tonight, he _____ (get) a good grade on the test.

6. If Maria _____ (improve) her computer skills, she _____ (be) happier at her job.

Lesson 5

1 WRITE sentences about Ed. Use *if* and the present or future form of the verb.

1. work late tonight? → (not) have to come in early tomorrow.

   If Ed works late tonight, he won't have to come in early tomorrow.

2. buy a new car → (not) have to ask his coworkers for a ride.

   _____

3. improve his English skills → get a promotion

   _____

4. arrive late for work again → get fired

   _____

5. save a lot of money → quit his job

   _____

6. take too many days off → (not) have any vacation time

   _____

2 MATH. Read the schedules. Calculate the time to answer the questions.

1. Angela has to work until 6:00 tonight. It takes her 30 minutes to drive home. It takes her one hour to make and eat dinner. Then she has to study for four hours before she goes to bed. What time will she go to bed tonight?

   _____

2. Angela has to work tomorrow at noon. It takes her 30 minutes to drive to work. She has to go grocery shopping first. It takes 20 minutes to drive to the grocery store and 20 minutes to drive back home. It takes 30 minutes to get her groceries and 20 minutes to put them away. What time does Angela have to go to the grocery store in the morning in order to get to work on time?

   _____

3. Angela has to work until 7:00 tomorrow night. After that, she is going out to dinner with some friends. She has to get gas first. It takes 10 minutes to drive to the gas station and five minutes to get gas. It takes 25 minutes to get to the restaurant from the gas station. What time will she be at the restaurant?

   _____

3 USE YOUR DICTIONARY. Write each verb in syllables. <u>Underline</u> the syllable that gets the most stress. Then practice the pronunciation with a partner.

1. invest: _in-<u>vest</u>_

2. improve: _____

3. commute: _____

4. retire: _____

Family Connection: Creating a Family Emergency Plan

1 MATCH the words and the meanings. Write the letters.

1. _____ communication

2. _____ contact person

3. _____ earthquake

4. _____ out of state

a. when the ground shakes

b. getting messages to people

c. in another state

d. a person to call or to talk to

2 READ the article.

Family Communication During an Emergency

What will you do if an emergency, such as a bad storm or an earthquake, happens in your community? Before an emergency happens, make a plan. An important part of any emergency plan is communication. You might not be with your family when an emergency happens. You might be at work and your children might be at school. What do you do?

First, choose a contact person to call. Think of a relative or friend who lives nearby. Make sure that you have this person's phone number. Also, think of an out-of-state relative or friend. This is a good idea if the emergency is everywhere in your state.

Then choose a place to go. Community centers and local schools are good meeting places. Make sure you know the phone number of your meeting place.

Then make family communication cards with this information for each family member. Family members should carry the card at all times. Give extra copies to your children's teachers, and keep a copy in your emergency kit at home. If you have an emergency, call your contact person. Tell your contact person that you are okay, and that you are going to the meeting place.

---

3 CIRCLE the correct words.

1. An important part of an emergency plan is **communication / transportation.**

2. You need a communication plan because family members usually **are / are not** together during the day.

3. A **neighbor / doctor** is a good emergency contact person.

4. You need an out-of-state contact in case the emergency is everywhere in your **community / state.**

5. **Community / Recycling** centers are good meeting places.

6. Keep extra copies of your emergency card in your **car / emergency kit.**

7. If you have an emergency, **call / go to** your contact person.

4 WRITE. Read Rosa's emergency plan. Fill out the card for her family.

Here's our plan: If there's an emergency, we're going to call Lara Jones, our next-door neighbor here in Los Angeles. Her number is 213-555-7869. If Lara isn't home, call Uncle Leo in Arizona. His number is 602-555-9345. Then go immediately to the Central Avenue School. We'll all meet there. The number at the school is 213-555-5684.

Family Emergency Communication Plan

Contact Name: _____

Telephone: _____

Out-of-State Contact Name: _____

Telephone: _____

Neighborhood Meeting Place: _____

Meeting Place Telephone: _____

5 REAL-LIFE LESSON

1. Make an emergency communication plan for your family. Write the names of people to call and places to meet. Find the phone numbers and write them here.

   _____ ( )_____

   _____

   _____ ( )_____

   _____

   _____ ( )_____

   _____

2. Make family communication cards for everyone in your family.

Community Connection: Using Emergency Services

1 **MATCH** the words with their meanings. Write the letters.

1. _____ collapsed

2. _____ insecticides

3. _____ illegal drugs

4. _____ inhaled

a. breathed in

b. fallen to the ground

c. chemicals that kill insects

d. drugs that are against the law

2 **READ** the information about calling a Poison Control Center.

http://www.poison-information.org/call

Calling a Poison Control Center

An important emergency service is the Poison Control Center. Every community in the United States has a Poison Control Center. The telephone number is **1-800-222-1222**. If you or a family member swallows, breathes, or touches a poison, call this number immediately. Someone will give you instructions and any other help you need. Do not call the Poison Control Center if the person has collapsed or has stopped breathing. In this case, you should call 911.

Examples of poisons are:

• overdose of prescription medicines and illegal drugs

• household cleaners, such as bleach

• chemicals at work or in the environment, such as insecticides

• insect and animal bites, for example, snake bites

What should you do if you or someone you know swallows, breathes, or touches a poison?

• If someone has swallowed the wrong medicine or too much medicine, call 1-800-222-1222 immediately.

• If someone has inhaled poison, first take the person outside, away from the poison. Then call 1-800-222-1222.

• If someone gets poison on their skin, first take off any clothing that has the poison on it. Then call 1-800-222-1222.

• If someone gets poison in the eyes, first put running water in the person's eyes for 15 to 20 minutes. Then call 1-800-222-1222.

3 **MATCH** the information from Activity 2. Write the letters. Then write sentences with *if*.

1. ___b___ someone gets poison in his eyes
2. _____ someone swallows the wrong medicine
3. _____ someone gets poison on her skin
4. _____ someone collapses
5. _____ someone inhales a poison

a. call 911
b. ~~put running water in his eyes for 15 to 20 minutes~~
c. first take him outside
d. call the Poison Control Center
e. first take off any clothing that has the poison on it

1. __If someone gets poison in his eyes, you put running water in his eyes for__ __15 to 20 minutes.__

2. _____

3. _____

4. _____

5. _____

4 **MATCH** the emergency pictures with the words. Write the letters.

| a. a hospital | b. call 911 | ~~c. police~~ | d. poison | e. fire |

1. ___c___   2. _____   3. _____   4. _____   5. _____

5 **REAL-LIFE LESSON.** Make list of emergency numbers in your community.

Police: _____

Fire Department: _____

Poison Control Center: _____ *1-800-222-1222* _____

Hospital: _____

Family member/Friend (name): _____

Other: _____

Career Connection: Giving Directions

1 **READ** the conversation. <u>Underline</u> the words that show the order of the steps.

> *A:* Hey, Rick, can you explain how to set up voice mail on my new phone?
>
> *B:* Sure, Mike. <u>First</u>, you call the voice mail company. That's 1-888-555-9786.
>
> *A:* Okay…
>
> *B:* Then you enter your extension number. Your extension number is the last three numbers on your employee time card.
>
> *A:* Okay…
>
> *B:* After that, you enter your password.
>
> *A:* Okay…
>
> *B:* The next step is to record your greeting. You know, "This is Mike. Leave me a message and I'll get back to you. . ."
>
> *A:* Sure…
>
> *B:* Finally, call 1836 to check your greeting. If you like it, you're done!
>
> *A:* Great! Thanks!

2 **WRITE.** Think of an activity with steps. Write the steps.

Activity: _____

1. _____
2. _____
3. _____
4. _____
5. _____

3 **PRACTICE.** Tell a partner how to do the activity above. Use the step words in the box.

first	then	next	after that	the next step is	finally

4 **REAL-LIFE LESSON.** Think of three activities you can learn that will help you at work or school. Write the names of people who can help you learn each one. Ask the people for directions.

Activities	People who can help
_____	_____
_____	_____
_____	_____

5 **EDIT.** There are six mistakes in the paragraph. Find them and correct them.

Employees sometimes have trouble getting all of their work done. If this happen^s to you,
what should you do? First, try to work more quickly or work more hours. If you comes in
earlier, you will to have more time to work without interruptions. Next, ask other employees for
advice. If they will have the same problem, they may have some good ideas. Finally, if you still
had too much work to finish, talk to your manager. He or she may to ask another employee to
help you do the work.

Technology Connection: Following Recorded Directions

A **LISTEN** to the recording. Write the number in the blank.

WCD, 46

1. To set up new Comweb service, press _____.

2. To report a problem with your Internet service, press _____.

3. For questions about your bill, press _____.

B **LISTEN.** Read the situations. Listen again. Write the number in the blank.

1. Your new friend works at Comweb Internet Service. You want to meet him for lunch.

   You press _____.

2. You made a repair appointment for Saturday morning, but now you are going on a

   trip that day. You press _____.

3. You want to know if Comweb has a Web design service. You press _____.

Practice Test

LISTENING: Listen to the voice mail message and the conversation. Then listen to the question. Choose the correct answer.

1. Ⓐ   Ⓑ   Ⓒ

2. Ⓐ   Ⓑ   Ⓒ

LISTENING: Listen to the conversation. Then choose the correct answer.

3. What does the young man need help with?
    A. buying a ticket
    B. finding a train station
    C. getting money

4. What does the man want to buy?
    A. a round-trip bus ticket
    B. a round-trip train ticket
    C. a one-way train ticket

5. Which is correct?
    A. The man is paying with a credit card.
    B. The man doesn't have any money.
    C. The man is paying with cash.

GRAMMAR: Choose the correct word or phrase to complete each sentence.

What (6) _____ I (7) _____ if I want to make an outside call?

6. A. did
    B. does
    C. doing
    D. do

7. A. did
    B. do
    C. doing
    D. does

8. What will you do if you _____ your job?
    A. will lose
    B. lost
    C. losing
    D. lose

If Lara (9) _____ healthier food, she (10) _____ weight.

9. A. eat
    B. eats
    C. ate
    D. eating

10. A. won't gain
     B. will
     C. gain
     D. gaining

VOCABULARY: Choose the best word or phrase to complete the sentence.

11. To make an outside call, press 9 and then _____ the number you want.
     A. use
     B. click
     C. dial
     D. do

12. *A:* I can't get this paper out of the printer.
     B: When the paper _____, turn off the power.
     A. jams
     B. runs
     C. unplugs
     D. presses

13. I want to know more about computers, so I'm going to take a class and ____ my skills.
    A. commute
    B. invest
    C. improve
    D. retire

14. Jake is going to ____ soon. He's going to stop working on his 60th birthday.
    A. commute
    B. retire
    C. invest
    D. improve

15. If I don't ____, I'll gain weight.
    A. keep fit
    B. get stuck
    C. make sure
    D. run out

READING: Read. Choose the correct answer.

Dog Calls 911

San Diego, CA.— On Monday, June 20, a five-year-old dog named Bo saved her owner's life.

Bo and her owner, Jack Owen, were walking in downtown San Diego when Owen collapsed. Owen has diabetes and his blood sugar was very low.

"I am alive today because of Bo," Owen said. Owen taught Bo to call 911 on his cell phone in an emergency. He set the number 9 on his cell phone to dial 911 and he taught Bo to bite down on it. Bo saw Owen collapse on Monday, and she found the cell phone in Owen's pocket. Then she bit down on the number 9, and an ambulance came immediately.

Most people should not set one number to call 911. If you do, you might call it accidentally. But for Owen, it was a good idea—it saved his life.

16. Who called 911?
    A. Diego
    B. Jack
    C. Owen
    D. Bo

17. Who is Bo?
    A. a man
    B. a dog
    C. a 911 operator
    D. an ambulance driver

18. Owen taught Bo to ____.
    A. dial 9 with her nose in an emergency
    B. dial 9 with her foot in an emergency
    C. say "Call 911" in an emergency
    D. dial 9 with her mouth in an emergency

19. What did Bo do?
    A. She found the cell phone and dialed 9.
    B. She found an ambulance.
    C. She found the cell phone and dialed 911.
    D. She set the number 9 to call 911.

20. It's usually not a good idea ____.
    A. to keep your cell phone in your pocket
    B. for dogs to call 911
    C. to call 911 if you collapse
    D. to set one number to call 911

Lesson 1

1   **COMPLETE** the sentences. Use the phrasal verbs in the box. Mari and Luis are moving to a new apartment. These are the things Mari has to do.

drop off	figure out	fill out	~~look over~~	pick out	turn in

1   First, I need to _look over_ the lease and sign it.

2   Luis will _____ the lease at the landlord's office later.

3   I must remember to _____ the keys to our old apartment.

4   Then I need to _____ how to move the furniture.

5   Luis is going to _____ a change-of-address form at the post office.

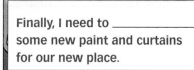

6   Finally, I need to _____ some new paint and curtains for our new place.

2   **REWRITE** the sentences. Use phrasal verbs from Activity 1. Change the underlined words to pronouns.

1. I need to read <u>the lease</u> carefully.   _I need to look it over._ _____

2. Please complete <u>this application</u>. _____

3. I need to choose <u>a lamp</u>. _____

4. You can leave <u>your package</u> at my house. _____

5. Can you help me solve <u>this problem</u>? _____

6. Please give back <u>your name card</u> when you leave. _____

Lesson 2

1 **READ** the sentences. Which phrasal verbs have an object? (Circle) *Object* or *No object*. If there is an object in the sentence, underline it.

1. Can you help me put <u>my new lamp</u> together?   (Object) / No object
2. Please come over to my house this weekend.   Object / No object
3. I ran into an old school friend at the post office today.   Object / No object
4. I'm going to stop by on my way to work.   Object / No object
5. I can't figure out this computer.   Object / No object

2 **COMPLETE** the paragraph. Use the phrasal verbs in the box. Decide if they need an object or not. Use a pronoun if they need an object.

come over	figure out	hook up	put away	put together	~~set up~~

Moving to a new apartment is a lot of work! There are boxes all over the place. First, I have to unpack my aquarium and (1) _____*set it up*_____ My poor fish are swimming in a plastic container right now. Then I have to find my computer and (2) _____ because I need to check my e-mail right away. Next, I have to take out the dishes and

(3) _____. I bought a new sofa, but it's in pieces so I have to

(4) _____ how to (5) _____.

Finally, I have to call all my friends so they can (6) _____ and we can

have a party!

3 **USE YOUR DICTIONARY.** Use your dictionary to find the meanings of these phrasal verbs. Write an example sentence. Find out if the verb is separable or inseparable. Does it have an object or not?

Phrasal verb	Example	Separable / inseparable	Object / No object
1. turn down	*She turned down my invitation.*	separable	object
2. put off			
3. get ahead			
4. look after			

Lesson 3

1 LISTEN to the beginning of a conversation. Then listen for the next best sentence. Fill in the circle for the correct answer.

1. Ⓐ Ⓑ Ⓒ
2. Ⓐ Ⓑ Ⓒ
3. Ⓐ Ⓑ Ⓒ

2 LISTEN to the conversation between a tenant and a landlord. What things are they going to do? Complete the chart.

The tenant is going to...	The landlord is going to...
paint the walls	

3 MATCH the questions with the answers. Write the letters.

1. How much is the rent? _____

2. Is the apartment available now? _____

3. Can I come over and take a look? _____

4. Can I move in right away? _____

5. Do you mind if I bring my dog? _____

a. Yes. The address is 28 Filbert Street.

b. You can move in on Monday.

c. It's $550 per month.

d. I'm sorry. Pets are not allowed.

e. Yes, it is.

4 PRACTICE. Make up your own conversation with a landlord. Write the conversation in your notebook. Practice with a partner.

5 PRONUNCIATION. Listen and write the next line in each conversation. Write the full forms of *want to, have to,* or *going to.*

1. *Tenant:* Can I move in tomorrow?

   Landlord: _____

2. *Tenant:* Is the apartment available now?

   Landlord: _____

3. *Landlord:* Can you drop off the lease tomorrow?

   Tenant: _____

Culture and Communication: Levels of Formality

1 READ these ways to start a conversation. Practice them with a partner. Use appropriate intonation.

Forms of Address	
Formal	**Informal**
Good morning, Mr./Ms. Andersen. May I speak with Professor Burton, please? How are you, Dr. Andrews?	Hi, Kathy! Hey, you guys! How's it going? What's up?

Culture Tip

In friendly, informal situations, most people will ask you to use their first names. In formal situations, such as job interviews or business meetings, you might have to use the person's title (Dr., Professor, Mr., or Ms.) unless they invite you to use their first name. Some teachers may ask you to use their first names in class. If you aren't sure, you should use the title or ask the teacher how he or she would like to be addressed. Most teachers will address their students by their first names.

2 READ these conversations. Talk with a partner. Are the conversations formal or informal? Who do you think is speaking?

1. *A:* Good morning. May I speak with Professor Larson, please?
   B: Yes, certainly. Who's calling, please?
   A: This is Carlos Gomez.

   Who do you think is speaking?   a. student and parent   b. student and teacher   c. two friends

2. *A:* Hey, Marta. How's it going?
   B: Not bad. Want to come over tomorrow night?
   A: Sure, what time?

   Who do you think is speaking?   a. student and parent   b. student and teacher   c. two friends

3 WRITE a conversation for each of the situations.

1. You see your friend standing at the bus stop as you are driving past, and you stop. Your friend's name is Lisa Martinez. Offer her a lift.

2. You want to speak to Professor Philips about a late assignment. You telephone her office and speak to the secretary. Make an appointment.

Lesson 4

1 MATCH the problems with the requests.

1. My apartment is too hot.
2. The stairs are dangerous.
3. My shower doesn't work.
4. I bought a new ceiling light.
5. The fire extinguishers are old.
6. I'm allergic to chemicals.

a. Replace the showerhead.
b. Install an air conditioner.
c. Remove the old light fixture.
d. Inspect the safety equipment.
e. Don't spray extermination chemicals.
f. Repair the railing.

2 WRITE. Use the words to write requests as reported speech.

1. she / ask / me / replace the showerhead
   She asked me to replace the showerhead.

2. he / tell / her / install an air conditioner
   _____

3. they / ask / him / remove the light fixture
   _____

4. we / tell / them / inspect the safety equipment
   _____

5. I / tell / him / don't repair the railing
   _____

3 REWRITE these requests as reported speech.

1. (she, us) Please be quiet.
   She told us to be quiet.

2. (they, us) Don't remove the smoke detectors.
   _____

3. (he, me) Please install a new showerhead.
   _____

4. (I, him) Please repair the broken window.
   _____

5. (he, them) Don't make too much noise.
   _____

Lesson 5

1 **READ** the paragraph. Cross out the words in italics. Replace them with words with the same meaning from the box.

inspect	~~install~~	pick out	remove	repair	replace

When I moved into my new apartment, I asked the landlord to

install

(1) ~~put in~~ an air conditioner and to (2) *fix* the broken window. I also

asked him to (3) *change* the locks on the door and (4) *check* the smoke

detectors to see if they are working. I asked my friend to help me

(5) *take down* the old-fashioned light fixtures. Then I asked my mother

to (6) *choose* some new curtains. She told me to buy a new carpet, too.

2 **MATH.** Calculate the costs of rent and moving.

1. Olga is moving to a new apartment. The rent on her old apartment was $750 a month. The rent on her new apartment is $600. How much will she save per year? _____

2. Olga has to pay one month's deposit and three months' rent in advance. How much does she have to pay? _____

3. Olga needs to rent a truck to move her furniture and boxes. The truck costs $25 per day, plus $30 for gas, and $25 for insurance. How much will the truck cost for one day? _____

3 **READ.** Which word does <u>not</u> go with the verb? Circle the answer.

1. install   ceiling fan / air conditioner / light fixture / curtains

2. replace   bathroom / stove / smoke detector / carpet

3. repair   air conditioner / light bulb / railing / toilet

4. pick out   curtains / carpet / milk / cabinets

5. hook up   cable / electricity / computer / phone

6. turn in   homework / keys / rent / report

Family Connection: Opening a Bank Account

1 **MATCH** these banking terms with their meanings. Write the letters.

1. __e__ A savings account
2. ____ A checking account
3. ____ A joint account
4. ____ A deposit
5. ____ A withdrawal
6. ____ An ATM card
7. ____ Direct debit
8. ____ Direct deposit

a. It does not give you interest, but you can write checks.

b. Your salary goes directly into your account every month.

c. You can use this to get cash or make deposits.

d. An account for more than one person.

e. ~~It gives you interest on your money.~~

f. You put money into the bank.

g. You take money out of the bank.

h. Utility bills or mortgage payments are paid directly from your account every month.

2 **READ.** Fill in the check and the deposit slip.

Mr. and Mrs. Grant just moved to East River. They decided to open a bank account in their new town. They wrote a check for $500 from their old bank account to open the new account. Complete the check and the deposit slip.

Victor and Emily Grant
23 Pine Place
Lakeview, TX 75009

Family Bank   432

Date: _____

Pay to the Order of _Victor and Emily Grant_____ $ [   ]

_____ dollars

For _to open a checking account_____

⑈012345⑈ ⑆123456543⑆ ⑈234567

Victor and Emily Grant
711 Rose Street
East River, TX 78642

Deposit Ticket
_789654_

Date: _____
Deposits may not be available for immediate withdrawl.

_____
Sign here for cash receipt.

East River Bank

054321   192837465   789654

Cash		
Checks		
Total		
Less Cash Received		
Total Deposit		

3 **COMPLETE** the application with your information.

EAST RIVER BANK ACCOUNT APPLICATION

You will need to have the following information to complete the process today:

1. Your social security or tax ID number.
2. Your driver's license or ID card issued by a state Department of Motor Vehicles.

Account selection

Please select the account you would like to open.

☐ Savings   ☐ Checking

Type of application

☐ Individual   ☐ Joint

Amount of deposit $ [   ]

Your personal information

_____

Title   First Name   Middle Name   Last Name

Social security number: _____ – _____ – _____

Date of birth (MM/DD/YY): _____ _____ _____

Joint account holder information

_____

Title   First Name   Middle Name   Last Name

Home telephone: _____

E-mail address: _____

Services required: ☐ checks   ☐ ATM card   ☐ direct deposit   ☐ direct debit

---

4 **REAL-LIFE LESSON.** Go to two or three banks (or look them up online) and get information about banking services. Make a list of services offered. Which of these services would you like to use? Which ones would you prefer not to use? Why?

Community Connection: Organizing a Community Project

1 READ the article. What is the main topic?

    a. how to repair your home   **b.** how to work together   **c.** how to get help

http://www.localnews.net

COMMUNITY NEWS ONLINE

Neighbors Work Together in East River Community

1   Strong winds damaged many of the homes in the East River community last winter. "Most of us did not have home-owner's insurance," says Frank Colman, "and we couldn't afford to pay for repairs to our roofs, walls, and fences. Some of us had leaks in our ceilings and broken windows. Our heating bills went up. It was very hard."

2   The neighbors of this community decided to get together and find out what they could do to help each other. Frank Colman organized a neighborhood meeting. At the meeting, residents made a list of repairs. Then they made a list of skills that were available in the community. Frank knows how to mend fences, for example, and Terry Cisneros, his neighbor, is good at plastering and painting. They made a list of how much time each person was able to give to the project.

3   "We couldn't do all the repairs ourselves, but we contacted a construction company. They're not interested in one small job, but when we told them we had several jobs lined up for them, we got a better deal," Frank says. Frank also asked some nonprofit organizations to help. "They donated

construction materials, and some volunteers came to help us. They told us to use better insulation to make our homes more energy efficient."

4   "We all got along together because we had to work together," says Terry Cisneros. Now the residents of East River are happy to have safe, warm, and dry homes. They have repaired their homes, but more important than that, they have strengthened their community.

2 READ the article again. Then read the main ideas below. Match the main ideas with the paragraphs. Write the number of the paragraph.

_____ The residents of East River need a lot of repairs to their homes.

_____ East River residents now have better homes and a better community.

_____ The neighbors shared their resources and their time.

_____ They asked some other organizations to help them.

3 ANSWER the questions.

1. Why did many homes in East River need repairs?

_____

2. How did the neighbors identify everyone's skills and plan what to do?

_____

3. Who did Frank ask to help them?

_____

4. What kind of help did they get from nonprofit organizations?

_____

5. Why is their community stronger now?

_____

6. What is the main idea of the article? Write one sentence.

_____

4 READ the information below. Write a letter to a nonprofit organization. Explain the problem and ask them to donate some money or construction materials to help rebuild your home.

Some floods damaged your home last spring. The house needs repairs to the walls and the basement. You don't have money or anyone to help you repair your home. Write to Rebuilding Together, a nonprofit organization, and ask for their help.

5 REAL-LIFE LESSON. Find out about nonprofit organizations where you can volunteer your time and skills, or get help for your community. Go online and find Rebuilding Together or Habitat for Humanity. Find the address of the branch or office closest to you.

Career Connection: Asking for a Transfer

1 **MATCH** the reasons for asking for a job transfer with the situations. Write the letters.

a.	Martina works in Houston. She is going to study at a college in El Paso.
b.	Amy's husband got transferred from Chicago to Washington, D.C.
c.	Teresa has back problems and needs a job where she doesn't have to stand all day.
d.	~~Gino works as a store manager in California, but he wants a more interesting job.~~
e.	Frank has just bought a new home and he needs to earn more money.

1. __d__ Your job is boring or too easy.

2. _____ You want to get a promotion.

3. _____ You want to move to another city or country.

4. _____ Your husband or wife got a job in another city.

5. _____ Your present job is not good for your health.

2 **READ** the letter. Then write a letter asking for a transfer. Use your own information or a situation from Activity 1.

Human Resources
Friendly Insurance Co.
1359 West Avenue
Newtown, MI 48005

November 26, 2009

Dear Ms. Hanson:

The San Francisco office of Friendly Insurance Company is advertising the position of senior accountant. I would like to submit my resume for a transfer.

I have worked for Friendly Insurance Company for three years as an accountant and I have enjoyed my work here very much. At this time, I want to improve my professional skills with your company and take on more responsibility.

Thank you for your consideration. I look forward to continuing my work for this company.

Sincerely,

Harry Golombek

Harry Golombek
Accountant, Finances Department

4 **EDIT.** The paragraph has eight mistakes in vocabulary and grammar. Find the mistakes and correct them.

                                                    out

Ivan applied for a new job. He filled ~~up~~ the application form and dropped off it at the human resources office. Then he looked over the company information on their website. One week later, they asked him come to an interview. It took Ivan a long time to pick over the right suit and tie. His girlfriend told him to don't wear bright colors, so he chose a dark suit and a navy blue tie. He asked to his girlfriend to practice interviewing with him. She told to figure up some good questions asking at the interview.

Technology Connection: Find Directions Online

You can use the websites www.maps.google.com or www.mapquest.com to find the location of a place or to get driving directions. To get directions, first type in the address of the place you are starting from. Then type the address of the place you are going to. Then click "Get Directions."

1. Look at the search form and the directions.

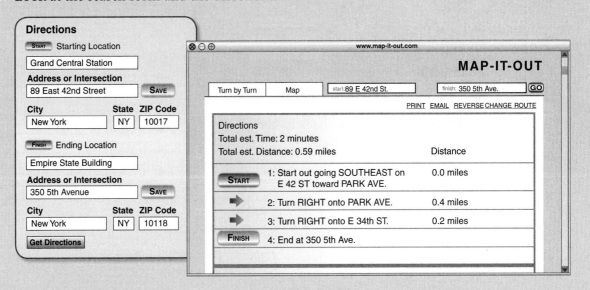

2. Find directions from your home to the nearest public library. Write them here.

_____

_____

Practice Test

LISTENING: Listen to the beginning of a conversation. Then listen for the next best sentence. Choose the correct answer.

1. Ⓐ   Ⓑ   Ⓒ

2. Ⓐ   Ⓑ   Ⓒ

LISTENING: Listen to the conversation. Then choose the correct answer.

3. Who is talking?
   A. a landlord and a tenant
   B. two tenants
   C. two landlords

4. What did the landlord come over to fix?
   A. the stair railing
   B. the light fixture
   C. the stove

5. What does the man want to ask the landlord to do?
   A. repair the stove
   B. replace the stove
   C. install an air conditioner

GRAMMAR: Choose the correct word or phrase to complete each sentence.

6. Monika needs new curtains. She's going to _____ today.
   A. pick out them
   B. pick them out
   C. pick it out
   D. pick out it

7. Fernando has to give the key back to his landlord. He needs to _____ today.
   A. turn in them
   B. turn them in
   C. turn it in
   D. turn in it

8. I saw my old school friend yesterday. I ran _____ .
   A. him into
   B. into him
   C. my friend into
   D. into it

9. She asked me _____ the window.
   A. repair
   B. repairing
   C. to repair
   D. I repair

10. They asked him _____ spray chemicals.
   A. to don't
   B. not to
   C. to not
   D. he didn't

VOCABULARY: Choose the best word to complete the sentence.

11. Monika needs to look ___ the lease.
    A. off
    B. over
    C. out
    D. in

12. They have to figure ___ how to move.
    A. off
    B. up
    C. in
    D. out

13. Can you drop ___ the form now?
    A. off
    B. out
    C. in
    D. up

14. This ceiling fan is broken. Can you ___ it?
    A. repair
    B. install
    C. inspect
    D. spray

15. This fire extinguisher is old. Can you ___ it?
    A. spray
    B. install
    C. repair
    D. replace

READING: Read. Choose the correct answer.

When you sign a lease, make sure you look it over carefully. If you do not understand something, ask the landlord to explain it.

It is important to inspect the apartment. Ask the landlord to make any repairs before you move in. Your apartment should be clean and in good condition at the time you sign the lease.

A good way to avoid disputes about repairs is complete a move-in checklist with your landlord. When you move out, you and the landlord will use this checklist to inspect the apartment again. The landlord will then return your security deposit. If you (or your guests) have caused any damage, the landlord will use your deposit to pay for the repairs.

16. What is the main topic of this article?
    A. asking your landlord to make repairs
    B. how to pay for repairs
    C. understanding rules for repairs
    D. learning about making repairs

17. What is the purpose of this article?
    A. advice for tenants
    B. advice for landlords
    C. advice for homeowners
    D. advice for building managers

18. Which is the best paraphrase of paragraph 2?
    A. Check the apartment before you move in.
    B. Ask the landlord to make repairs.
    C. Ask the landlord about the lease.
    D. You can ask about repairs later.

19. Which is the best paraphrase of paragraph 3?
    A. You cannot always get your deposit back.
    B. The landlord and tenant may disagree.
    C. A checklist will help prevent disagreements.
    D. You may have to pay for repairs.

20. The article says you should ___ before you move in.
    A. pay the security deposit
    B. sign the lease
    C. pay for the repairs
    D. check the apartment

Lesson 1

1 **COMPLETE** the sentences. Use the words in the box.

a bad mood	~~eat out~~	promoted
associate manager	exhausted	took out

1. We used to ___*eat out*___ once a week.

2. We're usually _____ by 7 P.M.!

3. The buses were often late. I was always in _____.

4. I _____ a loan and I bought a new car.

5. Before I got _____, I didn't have my own office.

6. I got my own office when I became _____.

2 **WRITE.** Combine the two sentences using a time clause and the time words in parentheses.

1. Pat used to socialize with her coworkers. She got promoted. (before)
   Pat used to socialize with her coworkers before she got promoted.

2. Sam and Carmen didn't eat out much. They had a baby. (after)
   _____

3. Tim bought a new car. He took out a loan. (as soon as)
   _____

4. She was often in a bad mood. She took the bus to work. (when)
   _____

5. Dan got a new office. He got promoted. (as soon as)
   _____

6. Hugo felt great. He became an associate manager. (when)
   _____

Lesson 2

1 **REWRITE** the sentences using gerunds.

1. After he graduated from high school, Sam left home.

   After graduating from high school, Sam left home.

2. Before she started college, she worked for one year.

   _____

3. Tony took out a loan before he started business school.

   _____

4. After she quit her job, Lina set up her own company.

   _____

5. Ana got engaged to Omar after she finished college.

   _____

6. I didn't quit my job after I had a baby.

   _____

2 **COMPLETE** the sentences. Write the answers in the crossword puzzle.

Across

4. Tony got _____ last week. Now he's a manager.

5. Amy and Dan got _____ in 2010, and got married in 2011.

7. We don't see our friends much. We're too tired to _____!

Down

1. He needed money for business school and won a _____.

2. I'm always in a bad _____ when the bus is late.

3. Sue took out a _____ because she wants to buy a car.

5. I'm very tired. In fact, I'm _____.

6. After he _____ his job, he started a company.

Lesson 3

WCD, 54

1 **LISTEN** to the question. Then listen to the conversation. Listen to the question again. Fill in the circle for the correct answer.

1. Ⓐ   Ⓑ   Ⓒ
2. Ⓐ   Ⓑ   Ⓒ
3. Ⓐ   Ⓑ   Ⓒ

2 **WRITE** the lines of the conversation in the correct order.

She got her bachelor's degree!

Yes. And after she got her degree, she got a scholarship to business school!

~~Hi, Deb. Did you hear about Pia?~~

No, what happened?

Good for her!

A: ___Hi, Deb. Did you hear about Pia?_____

B: _____

A: _____

B: _____

A: _____

3 **PRACTICE** the conversation in Activity 2 with a partner.

WCD, 55

4 **LISTEN.** Is the speaker asking a question or checking meaning? Check ☑ the correct box.

1. ☐ Ask a question   ☐ Check meaning

2. ☐ Ask a question   ☐ Check meaning

3. ☐ Ask a question   ☐ Check meaning

4. ☐ Ask a question   ☐ Check meaning

5. ☐ Ask a question   ☐ Check meaning

Culture and Communication: Asking for Clarification

1 **READ** the job interview conversations.

> **Culture Tip**
>
> It's okay to ask questions when you don't understand something, especially during a job interview.
>
> **Useful Expressions**
>
> (I'm sorry.) Did you say (that)…?
> Are you saying (that)…?
> Do you mean (that)…?
> When you say…, do you mean (that)…?

1. **A:** So Dan, we don't have enough people here. We're looking for someone who is free right now.

   B: I'm sorry, Ms. Green. Did you say that you need someone who can start the job right away?

   A: That's right.

2. **A:** And in addition to your salary, you can get a bonus each year if you reach your goals.

   B: When you say *bonus*, are you saying that I can get additional money each year if I meet my goals?

   A: Absolutely.

2 **WRITE** answers to the questions.

1. In Conversation 1, what doesn't Speaker B understand? _____

   Underline the expression the speaker uses to ask for clarification.

2. In Conversation 2, what word doesn't Speaker B understand? _____

   Underline the expression the speaker uses to ask for clarification.

3. What is a bonus? _____

3 **PRACTICE.** Have a conversation with a partner. Speaker A chooses one of the topics below and explains it to Speaker B. Speaker B asks for clarification of anything he or she doesn't understand. Use the expressions in the Culture Tip box above. Then exchange roles.

   Topics

1. Where did you study before you joined this class?

2. Where did you live when you were a child?

3. What did you do after you went home yesterday?

Lesson 4

1 COMPLETE the sentences. Use the words in the box.

consult	GED	~~mortgage~~	repay
down payment	go back to work	relocate	tuition

1. We're going to pay off our ___mortgage___. After that, we're going to _____ to Los Angeles. I have always wanted to live in Los Angeles!

2. I'll have more money after I graduate, so I'll _____ my loan then.

3. I have an appointment to talk to an advisor, but I need money to pay for school.

   I'll _____ with my advisor as soon as I get the money for _____.

4. I'm going to save money to make my first payment on a home. I'll need about $40,000 for

   the _____.

5. I'm going to get my _____ and then I'm going to go to college.

6. I'll _____ when my children are older.

2 WRITE the correct verb forms.

1. We're going to pay off our mortgage as soon as we _____save_____ (save) enough money.

2. After Leon _____ (get) his high school diploma, he's going to attend classes at a community college.

3. Slava _____ (go) back to work when her children start school.

4. Hassan _____ (not register) for classes until he consults an advisor.

5. Will Francisco relocate to Sacramento after he _____ (sell) his house?

3 WRITE. Read the plans. Then write sentences. Use the words in parentheses.

1. Ana's plan
   1. get a GED
   2. go to college

2. Rob's plan
   1. save some money
   2. make a down payment on a home

3. Lara's plan
   1. borrow some money for school
   2. register for classes

4. Alan's plan
   1. get a job
   2. repay his loan

1. (after) ___After she gets a GED, Ana will go to college.___

2. (as soon as) _____

3. (not. . . until) _____

4. (when) _____

Lesson 5

1 COMPLETE the paragraph. Make certain or possible sentences. Use the verbs in parentheses and *going to, will, may, might,* or *could.*

Raul wants to be a nurse. First, he (1) __is going to get__ (get, certain) his high school diploma.

Then he (2) _____ (apply, certain) to college. He (3) _____ (visit, certain) a lot

of colleges in the state. He (4) _____ (live, possible) with his parents while attending

college, or he (5) _____ (relocate, possible) to San Diego and live with his uncle. He

(6) _____ (work, certain) part time while he's in college. He (7) _____

(get, possible) a job in a hospital. He (8) _____ (get, possible) a loan for his tuition, but

he (9) _____ (have, certain) a good job after he graduates. He (10) _____

(repay, certain) the loan after he gets his first job.

2 MATH. Solve the problems.

1. Mari compared two Web design courses. One is at Bay City College and costs $450 for 4 weeks, two hours a week. The other course is at Simpson Technical College and costs $400 for 6 weeks, one hour a week. Which course costs less per hour?_____

2. Luis compared two English courses. One is at Greenfield Community College and costs $650 for 15 weeks, three hours a week. The other course is at River City Community College and costs $650 for 6 weeks, six hours a week. Which course costs less per hour?_____

3. Rob compared two music courses. One is at River City Music School and costs $550 for 14 weeks, two hours a week. The other course is at Sandford Community College and costs $950 for 12 weeks, six hours a week. Which course costs less per hour?_____

3 USE YOUR DICTIONARY. Use the words and phrases in the box to answer the questions.

get a GED	**go back** to work	**make** a down payment	**pay off** a mortgage

1. What kind of words are the bold words? ☐ nouns ☐ verbs

2. What kind of words are the underlined words? ☐ nouns ☐ verbs

3. Find at least one more phrase with each of the bold words.

get : _____

go back: _____

make: _____

pay off: _____

Family Connection: Completing a W-4 Form

1 **READ** about W-4 forms.

Americans pay income taxes two ways: 1) Employers take money from your paycheck and pay the government directly; 2) You pay the government directly one time each year if your employer did not pay enough for you during the year.

When you start a new job, your employer will ask you to fill out a W-4 form. A W-4 form tells your employer how much money to take out of your salary for your income taxes. It's like a guess.

When you fill out the W-4 form, you tell about your dependents. Dependents are the people you live with and take care of, such as your children. You get deductions from your income taxes for your dependents and for yourself. You also get deductions for money that you pay for childcare.

A W-4 worksheet helps you add up your total number of deductions. Here's an example: Serena Jones is starting a new job. She's married and she has two children. She pays for childcare for her children. Here's how Serena filled out the worksheet:

A Enter "1" for yourself.   _1_

B Enter "1" for your spouse. You may enter "0" if you are   _0_
married and your spouse works.

C Enter the number of dependents that you have.   _2_

D Enter "1" if you spend at least $1,500 on childcare in a year.   _1_

E Add lines A, B, C, and D.   _4_

Here's what Serena Jones's W-4 form looks like:

----- Cut here and give Form W-4 to your employer. Keep the top part for your records. -----

Form **W-4**	Employee's Withholding Allowance Certificate	OMB No. 1545-0074
Department of the Treasury Internal Revenue Service	► **Whether you are entitled to claim a certain number of allowances or exemption from withholding is subject to review by the IRS. Your employer may be required to send a copy of this form to the IRS.**	20**10**

1 Type or print your first name and middle initial. Serena L.	Last name Jones		2 Your social security number 012 : 34 : 5678
Home address (number and street or rural route) 5932 Landis Street		3 ☐ Single ☑ Married ☐ Married, but withhold at higher Single rate. **Note.** If married, but legally separated, or spouse is a nonresident alien, check the "Single" box.	
City or town, state, and ZIP code San Diego, CA 92105		4 If your last name differs from that shown on your social security card, check here. You must call 1-800-772-1213 for a replacement card. ► ☐	

5	Total number of allowances you are claiming (from line **H** above **or** from the applicable worksheet on page 2)	**5**	4
6	Additional amount, if any, you want withheld from each paycheck	**6** $	
7	I claim exemption from withholding for 2008, and I certify that I meet **both** of the following conditions for exemption.		

  • Last year I had a right to a refund of **all** federal income tax withheld because I had **no** tax liability **and**
  • This year I expect a refund of **all** federal income tax withheld because I expect to have **no** tax liability.

  If you meet both conditions, write "Exempt" here . . . . ► | 7 |

Under penalties of perjury, I declare that I have examined this certificate and to the best of my knowledge and belief, it is true, correct, and complete.
Employee's signature
(Form is not valid
unless you sign it.) ► *Serena L. Jones*   **Date ►**

8 Employer's name and address (Employer: Complete lines 8 and 10 only if sending to the IRS.)	9 Office code (optional)	10 Employer identification number (EIN)

For Privacy Act and Paperwork Reduction Act Notice, see page 2. | Cat. No. 10220Q | Form **W-4** (2010)

---

2 **READ** the W-4 form in Activity 1 again. Check *True* or *False*. Correct the false statements.

	True	False
1. Your employer needs your W-4 form in order to know how many children you have.	☐	☐
2. Your W-4 form lists the number of dependents that you have.	☐	☐
3. You can get a deduction if you pay for childcare.	☐	☐
4. Serena Jones is taking one deduction for her husband.	☐	☐
5. Serena Jones is taking 2 deductions for her children.	☐	☐
6. Serena Jones's total number of dependents is 4.	☐	☐

3 **REAL-LIFE LESSON.** Answer the W-4 worksheet questions for yourself. Then fill out the W-4 form.

A Enter "1" for yourself. _____

B Enter "1" for your spouse. You may enter "0" if you are married and your spouse works. _____

C Enter the number of dependents that you have. _____

D Enter "1" if you spend at least $1,500 on childcare in a year. _____

E Add lines A, B, C, and D. _____

- - - - - - - - - - - - - - - - **Cut here and give Form W-4 to your employer. Keep the top part for your records.** - - - - - - - - - - - - - - - -

Form **W-4**

Department of the Treasury
Internal Revenue Service

Employee's Withholding Allowance Certificate

▶ **Whether you are entitled to claim a certain number of allowances or exemption from withholding is subject to review by the IRS. Your employer may be required to send a copy of this form to the IRS.**

OMB No. 1545-0074

20**10**

1 Type or print your first name and middle initial.	Last name	2 Your social security number

Home address (number and street or rural route)	3 ☐ Single ☐ Married ☐ Married, but withhold at higher Single rate. **Note.** If married, but legally separated, or spouse is a nonresident alien, check the "Single" box.
City or town, state, and ZIP code	4 If your last name differs from that shown on your social security card, check here. You must call 1-800-772-1213 for a replacement card. ▶ ☐

5	Total number of allowances you are claiming (from line **H** above **or** from the applicable worksheet on page 2)	5
6	Additional amount, if any, you want withheld from each paycheck	6 $
7	I claim exemption from withholding for 2008, and I certify that I meet **both** of the following conditions for exemption.	

  • Last year I had a right to a refund of **all** federal income tax withheld because I had **no** tax liability **and**
  • This year I expect a refund of **all** federal income tax withheld because I expect to have **no** tax liability.
  If you meet both conditions, write "Exempt" here . . . . ▶ | 7 |

Under penalties of perjury, I declare that I have examined this certificate and to the best of my knowledge and belief, it is true, correct, and complete.

Employee's signature
(Form is not valid
unless you sign it.) ▶

Date ▶

8 Employer's name and address (Employer: Complete lines 8 and 10 only if sending to the IRS.)	9 Office code (optional)	10 Employer identification number (EIN)

For Privacy Act and Paperwork Reduction Act Notice, see page 2. | Cat. No. 10220Q | Form **W-4** (2010)

Community Connection: Understanding Course Descriptions

1 CHECK ☑ your job skills. Do you have any of these skills?

- ☐ business English
- ☐ using business computer programs
- ☐ translating documents
- ☐ culinary arts (cooking for restaurants and hotels)
- ☐ website design

What other job skills do you have? _____

What job skills would you like to have? _____

2 READ the course descriptions in a community center brochure.

Did you know that the Bayview Community Center offers career advancement classes?

Right here in your own community center, you can:

☀ learn new job skills
☀ improve your job skills
☀ prepare for a new career

Here are some examples of the career advancement courses that we offer:

☀ **Business English Skills:** Would you like to improve your English skills at work? This course will help you speak, read, and write better business English.

☀ **Computer Skills:** Most jobs require computer skills. Do you know all the latest software? This course will teach you important business computer software for your career. Not for beginners.

☀ **Beginning Culinary Arts:** Do you like to cook? Would you like to work as a chef? This course will help you get started.

☀ **Beginning Website Design:** Prepare for a career as a website designer. Learn to create and maintain all types of websites.

☀ **Resume Writing Workshop:** Do you know how to write a resume that will get you a job? This workshop will teach you everything you need to know.

☀ **Translation:** Do you speak a second language? If so, you already have a special skill! Become a translator. Learn how to translate business and technical documents.

---

3 **WRITE** answers to the questions.

1. Which course(s) might help you start a new career? _____

   _____

2. Which course(s) might help you do better at the job you have now? _____

   _____

3. Which course(s) is/are for beginners? _____

   _____

4. For which course(s) do you need a special skill? _____

   _____

5. Which course might be important for getting any job? _____

   _____

4 **READ** about the people. Use the information from the community center brochure. Write the best course for each person.

1. Ana works at a hotel. She would like to be a manager. She speaks English well, but managers must be able to write reports.

   _____

2. Paolo would like to prepare for a new career. His hobby is cooking. He might like to work as a chef.

   _____

3. Teresa works in an office. She speaks Spanish. She's thinking of changing jobs.

   _____

4. Jason just finished high school. He loves computers, but he doesn't want a regular job in business. He thinks that he is a creative person.

   _____

5. Serena is a nurse. She wants to apply for a new job. She doesn't have a resume.

   _____

6. Alan works in an office. He wants to get a better job at his company. He has basic computer skills.

   _____

5 **REAL-LIFE LESSON.** Answer these questions. Share your answers with the class.

Does your community center have career advancement courses? If yes, which ones? If no, where in your community can you take career advancement courses?

Career Connection: Writing a Resume

1 **READ** Serena's resume.

5932 Landis Street   Phone (619)-555-4893
San Diego, CA 92105   E-mail SJones61@mail.com

Serena L. Jones

Objective   A position as a registered nurse in a hospital.

Experience   Licensed Practical Nurse: January 2005–Present
                   Chula Vista Community Hospital, Chula Vista, CA
                   • Managed patient care. Special skills include working with
                     pediatric and physical therapy patients.

                   Health Aide: February 1999 – March 2003
                   Sunnyside Senior Care, San Diego, CA
                   • Assisted residents: helped with daily activities such as eating,
                     dressing, and walking.
                   • Cooked for residents.

Education   San Diego State University B.S. Nursing
                   Costa Verde Community College LPN license
                   University High School High School Diploma

Skills   Speak fluent Spanish
                   Play piano

References   Available upon request.

2 **COMPLETE** the sentences. Circle the correct words.

1. Serena's resume includes her **age / phone number**.

2. Serena's resume **does / does not** include information about her family.

3. Her objective is the job that Serena **has now / wants**.

4. The **Experience / Skills** section shows Serena's past jobs.

5. The **Education / Experience** section lists Serena's schools.

6. Serena has **computer / music** skills.

 3 **THINK AND WRITE.** What kind of information do you put in a resume? What kind of information don't you put in a resume?

4 **REAL-LIFE LESSON.** Write a resume for yourself. Include your objective, your experience, your education, and your skills.

3 **EDIT.** Read Dan's description of his last job. Then read Serena's resume again. Rewrite Dan's information in the correct form for a resume.

> After I graduated, I worked at Trustcom in Tarzana, CA from June 2004 to May 2007. I was an administrative assistant. I answered phone calls and e-mails for four managers. I also made travel arrangements for all employees.

_____

_____

_____

 Technology Connection: Checking Credit Card Balances

Credit Card Tips

- Try not to make just the minimum payments—the smallest amounts you can pay. Instead, pay your balance—the total amount—each month. If you can't do that, pay as much as you can.
- Don't have too many cards.
- Always know your balance. You can check your balance on the phone or online.

WCD, 56

A **LISTEN** to the information about Jake's credit card. Match the numbers with the words.

1. _____ current balance   a. $25
2. _____ last statement balance   b. $1,200
3. _____ last payment   c. $800
4. _____ minimum payment   d. $550

B **LISTEN** again. Then write answers.

1. If Jake pays his total balance right now, how much must he pay? _____

2. Did Jake pay his total balance last month? _____

3. When did Jake pay his last bill? How much did he pay? _____

4. When should Jake pay his next bill? _____

Practice Test

LISTENING: Listen to the question. Listen to the conversation. Listen to the question again. Choose the correct answer.

1. (A)   (B)   (C)

2. (A)   (B)   (C)

🎧 WCD, 58 **LISTENING:** Listen to the conversation. Then choose the correct answer.

3. Why was getting promoted difficult for Ana?
   A. She has more money.
   B. She worries about her children.
   C. She has more work.

4. How did Ana feel before she got promoted?
   A. She worried about money.
   B. She worried about her coworkers.
   C. She worried about working late.

5. Why is money important to Ana?
   A. Now she can go to college.
   B. Now she can send her children to college.
   C. Now she can spend more time with her family.

GRAMMAR: Choose the correct word or phrase to complete each sentence.

6. After ____ to Los Angeles, Tina got engaged.
   A. moved
   B. moves
   C. moving
   D. move

Jack (7) ____ the loan after he (8) ____.

7. A. will repay
   B. repaid
   C. repaying
   D. repay

8. A. will graduate
   B. graduating
   C. graduates
   D. graduate

9. Before Joe ____ his driver's license, he took the bus to work.
   A. gets
   B. getting
   C. will get
   D. got

10. ____ from her job, she'll play golf all day.
    A. After she retire
    B. After she retires
    C. Before she retiring
    D. If she retired

VOCABULARY: Choose the best word or phrase to complete the sentence.

11. I ____ to buy a car.
    A. took out a loan
    B. made a down payment
    C. got a scholarship
    D. got engaged

12. Sue ____ at work. Now she's a manager.
    A. got a scholarship
    B. got engaged
    C. got a loan
    D. got promoted

13. *A:* Where is Jane from?

    B: Jane ____ in Denver.

    A. set up

    B. pay off

    C. grew up

    D. took out

14. Sam and Lina lived in Chicago before they ____ to San Diego.

    A. relocated

    B. repaid

    C. registered

    D. renewed

15. I need some help, so I'm going to ____ with an advisor before I start college.

    A. get

    B. relocate

    C. consult

    D. socialize

READING: Read. Choose the correct answer.

Bayview Community College • College Success Courses

College Success courses help students to prepare for success at Bayview Community College.

Section	Class Title	Day	Time	Credits	Start	End
CS 100-1	Study Skills	Th	6 P.M.–7:30 P.M.	1	1/24	5/29
CS 100-2	College Reading Skills	MWF	5:30 P.M.–7:30 P.M.	6	1/21	5/30
CS 100-3	College Writing Skills	MWF	10 A.M.–12:30 P.M.	6	1/21	5/30
CS 102-1	Critical Thinking	TTh	1:30 P.M.–3:00 P.M.	3	1/22	5/29
CS 102-2	Test Taking	MW	11 A.M.–12:30 P.M.	3	1/21	5/28

16. This schedule gives information about ____ at Bayview Community College.

    A. placement tests

    B. meeting with an advisor

    C. how to register for classes

    D. taking College Success courses

17. Lisa will take a class three times a week during the day. She will take ____.

    A. Test Taking

    B. College Reading Skills

    C. Study Skills

    D. College Writing Skills

18. Jack works during the day and he only needs one credit. He'll take ____.

    A. Test Taking

    B. College Reading Skills

    C. Study Skills

    D. College Writing Skills

19. Ana can only take classes at night and she needs 6 credits. She'll take ____.

    A. Study Skills

    B. College Reading Skills

    C. College Writing Skills

    D. Critical Thinking

20. Mark works on Wednesday morning and needs 3 credits. He will take ____.

    A. Critical Thinking

    B. Study Skills

    C. Test Taking

    D. College Reading Skills

Correlation Table

Student Book	Workbook
Pre-Unit	
2–5	2–5
Unit 1	
6–7	6
8–9	7
10–11	8–9
12–13	10
14–15	11
16–17	12–13
18–19	14–15
20	16–17
21	18–19
Unit 2	
22–23	20
24–25	21
26–27	22–23
28–29	24
30–31	25
32–33	26–27
34–35	28–29
36	30–31
37	32–33
Unit 3	
38–39	34
40–41	35
42–43	36–37
44–45	38
46–47	39
48–49	40–41
50–51	42–43
52	44–45
53	46–47
Unit 4	
54–55	48
56–57	49
58–59	50–51
60–61	52
62–63	53
64–65	54–55
66–67	56–57
68	58–59
69	60–61

Student Book	Workbook
Unit 5	
70–71	62
72–73	63
74–75	64–65
76–77	66
78–79	67
80–81	68–69
82–83	70–71
84	72–73
85	74–75
Unit 6	
86–87	76
88–89	77
90–91	78–79
92–93	80
94–95	81
96–97	82–83
98–99	84–85
100	86–87
101	88–89
Unit 7	
102–103	90
104–105	91
106–107	92–93
108–109	94
110–111	95
112–113	96–97
114–115	98–99
116	100–101
117	102–103
Unit 8	
118–119	104
120–121	105
122–123	106–107
124–125	108
126–127	109
128–129	110–111
130–131	112–113
132	114–115
133	116–117

Student Book	Workbook
Unit 9	
134–135	118
136–137	119
138–139	120–121
140–141	122
142–143	123
144–145	124–125
146–147	126–127
148	128–129
149	130–131
Unit 10	
150–151	132
152–153	133
154–155	134–135
156–157	136
158–159	137
160–161	138–139
162–163	140–141
164	142–143
165	144–145
Unit 11	
166–167	146
168–169	147
170–171	148–149
172–173	150
174–175	151
176–177	152–153
178–179	154–155
180	156–157
181	158–159
Unit 12	
182–183	160
184–185	161
186–187	162–163
188–189	164
190–191	165
192–193	166–167
194–195	168–169
196	170–171
197	172–173